Diary of a Bartender

Diary of a Bartender
Brooklyn to Big Sur, *a Life at Work*

Herb Evans

26 Letter Press
Big Sur, California

Diary of a Bartender, Brooklyn to Big Sur, a life at work
© 2019, Herb Evans

26 Letter Press
48510 Highway 1
Big Sur, CA 93920

ISBN: 978-1-950731-00-8

Introduction by Tom Birmingham
Cover Design by Ann Artz
Back Cover Photo by Tom Birmiongham

For information about bulk purchases, sales promotions,
fund-raising and educational needs -

26 Letter Press

Big Sur, California
www.bigsurarts.com
831.646.9000 | tom@bigsurarts.com

Herb Evans

Dedication

I dedicate this memoir to my three children and seven grand kids.

Illia Thompson started a memoir class and every Wednesday I put myself in the class and got encouragement.

I've had the support of my good friend, Steve Copeland for almost fifty years.

Bob Yuro has been my partner and friend since we met on Thirty Fourth Street in 1955.

Jim Swindle worked at bar with me at Alice's, and was an important part of my story.

At Nepenthe, I was exposed to Erin Gafill and Tom Birmingham, two artists, partners in life. They helped me edit and publish this book.

Marnie Sperry typed and helped edit.

I could list many at Nepenthe that kept asking, "How's the book coming along?"

Introduction -

If you've ever been lucky enough to perch on a bar stool and hear the tales of a great raconteur, you have an idea of what to expect in Herb Evans's memoir. He spins the stories that are the building blocks of his life, and leaves you to decide on their meaning.

He invites you to follow an improbable path from Brooklyn to Broadway, from the Village to the Coast, from Malibu to Big Sur. He places himself as a character actor in his own drama, with humility and gratitude for all he's had the opportunity to experience.

Herb's life is one of restlessness and resourcefulness. He can't look at an empty storefront without imagining how to turn it into a neighborhood joint. Where would you put the kitchen? How many seats could the bar fit? Could I put tables on the sidewalk? But once the doors are open, once the seats are filled and the guests are served, there is an itch that needs to be scratched. He is always looking to move on to the next place.

As a young man hustling Off-Off-Broadway parts

in the 50's and 60's, Herb worked at dozens of bars and restaurants. Before he was thirty, his first place Herb Evans Restaurant, put his name in lights, 185 feet long on Broadway at Sixty Fourth Street. If he'd stayed put, his name would have gone down with New York's most storied restaurateurs. But family and circumstances lured him to the West Coast.

Along with his oldest friend, Bob Yuro, he opened Alice's Restaurant, first in Westwood, and later on the pier in Malibu. Even though city life ran through his veins, he was no match for the siren song of Big Sur.

In the early 70's, Bill Fassett invited him to Big Sur to run his "Little hamburger joint, maybe you've heard of it? Nepenthe?" He came north hoping to tame the circus that was Nepenthe in those days. He worked there for years, with time out for other startups and ventures.

Throughout the years his number one commitment was to his family. He worked hard to succeed, to give his three kids the kind of stability he never found as a ten-year-old kid in Brooklyn, raising himself after his mother's passing

But to tell more would be to spoil the fun. Here, in *Diary of a Bartender*, Herb tells the tales and weaves the stories that made him the man he is.

Now, turn the page and begin...

Writing This Memoir

Writing this memoir started with the encouragement of my three kids - Shelley, Sam, and Kyle. They said they wanted to know what I was all about. I kept saying, "What you see is what you get."

It took a lot to get me here started.

How can I tell the story? Am I kidding? I never wrote anything in my life. Over these past few months, I've been documenting, experiencing things that I did from childhood to the present.

Lately, I realize that there's a lot I never took the time to feel, what I learned, what sent me in the direction that I went in.

Now I'm here, and I am feeling things that I never took the time to examine. I was fortunate to have teachers, not in formal education but in life. This feels like the beginning.

Herb Evans

A Really Cold November Day

On a really cold November day in New York City, 1955, the Greyhound bus pulled into the station. I grabbed my duffel bag, put on my pea coat, and went out onto Thirty Fourth Street.

There were wall-to-curb people rushing to somewhere. I took a deep breath and stood there a moment, and realized I had no idea where I was going.

I started walking west, picking up speed. I made it a game, dodging in and out of people without touching anyone. I got to Thirty Fourth and Seventh Avenue. There was a line of people wrapped around the block. They were waiting to get into Macy's Department Store.

I asked this guy what was going on. "They're hiring Christmas help, if you want a job, stand in line. You can cut in."

Nobody complained. It was so cold, people were sunk into their coats like turtles in their shells. It took about two hours to get an application and a quick interview.

My new friend Bob Yuro and I both got hired. We were told to come Monday morning for training, to have a clean shirt and pants. I could shop while I was in the biggest store in the city. I had three hundred bonus dollars from the Navy that should hold me for a couple of weeks.

Bob said, "See you Monday," and he disappeared down the stairs to get the subway. Now I had to find a place to live.

I just started walking up Eighth Avenue and I spotted a flashing neon sign on 5 Street. "Floral Studios" furnished rooms five to ten dollars a week. It felt strange, for the last 4 years I didn't do anything that I wasn't told to do. I loved the Navy, it was family.

I walked in. There was a guy sitting behind the desk, skinny, with a cigarette hanging out of his mouth and ashes falling on his chest.

"What do you want, kid?"

"I'd like to rent a five-dollar room."

"Okay, let's go up and take a look. Follow me."

We got into a cage, this was the elevator. He pulled the door shut and it started up, shaking and slow. It stopped on the third floor. I thought for sure the cable would snap.

Harry, that was his name, was calm and relaxed, let the ashes fall and was okay with it.

The room was clean, the bed had a thin mattress folded on sagging springs, a sink, dresser, a radiator, a single bare bulb hanging down at the center. An old shade covered the window, the kind you pull down and let it wind up.

I put the shade up and opened the window. The view was a brick wall, an air shaft. You had to look up to see the weather. The bathroom with shower was in the hall, shared by three rooms. A refrigerator was in the hall, also shared, but divided into compartments to fit a small milk and maybe an apple. I looked at Harry.

This was perfect, I was home. After signing a paper, I got the key.

I was hungry, so I went out to an automat.

These were restaurants that were like vending machines. You dropped a nickel or dime in and opened the glass door and took the plate out: ten cents for a vegetable, five cents for coffee, soups, pies, mostly ten or fifteen cents.

It was busy, seemed like people were getting in out of the cold.

After I ate I went home, really tired, just wanted to sleep. I was going to be okay. The first day I got a job, a place to sleep, and a friend. Looking forward to Monday.

This is the beginning of my new life. But I'm getting ahead of myself. Let me tell you a little of my early life.

Herb Evans

Sense Memories, Uninvited

Years of exhaust fumes of gas floating by in New York City.

Smells of boiled potatoes mixed with medicine and laundry, visiting Mom in hospital.

Smells of diesel oil circulating encased in a submarine.

Fresh cool wet of the ocean, first smell coming up.

Smells of French fries and grilled meat working in restaurants.

Redwoods, grass, and ocean in Big Sur.

Cleaning chemicals in cheap motels.

Frozen-stiff clothes coming off the line.

Wet burlap covering the ice being delivered.

Smells in hallways of apartment buildings, a mixture of different food cooking.

Faint sounds of radios, TVs, people talking, walking by in the city.

Seeing the waves of heat coming up from concrete.

Herb Evans

Early Days

Herb Evans

The Days of Radio

We used to play hockey in the street. Our roller skates had steel wheels and used to clamp onto our shoes. I always had my skate key handy.

I remember sitting on the floor in front of the console radio listening to my favorite shows. Friday night was a big one: *Gangbusters*.

The streets were empty, all my friends were inside. I can still hear the commercial: "Lava Lava Lava soap." I could see the picture as clear as day without a screen.

One of the favorites was *Lux Theater*. The dramatizations were so good. *Inner Sanctum* was as scary as any horror movie. If you wanted to know who knows? Well, *The Shadow Knows*.

Orson Welles broadcast a dramatization of *War of the Worlds*, a radio anthology series on The Mercury Theater. *War of the Worlds* was performed as a Halloween episode of the series on Sunday, October 30, 1938, and aired over the CBS Broadcasting System radio network.

It supposedly caused a panic. They started with simulated news flashes. I think radio was more pow-

erful than television. Nothing is as powerful as imagination. The door opens and your mind can take you
anywhere.

My friends and I made our own scooters. We'd
take a two by four, nail an old pair of skates on the
front and back. We'd take an orange crate, nail it on
the front. Take two slats off the crate and nail them
on so they would be the handles.

These scooters were perfect to carry groceries
home, good to carry school books. There weren't
any backpacks. There weren't any shopping carts at
the A&P Markets, so this was a great way to get tips
helping people with bundles to their cars.

Marbles were a great currency. I used to dream
of having a roomful of them. My friend Joey Schutz
and Tommy Maziotti and I made up a gambling
game. We took a shoe box, cut holes so a marble
could fit through, then we'd draw a chalk line in the
middle of the street.

The box would be next to the curb. We would be
the bank, going to other blocks, kids would try their
luck rolling marbles to get them through the holes.
If you did, you got two back.

The odds were with us. We were getting lots of
marbles.

Orange crates were really useful. There wasn't
any cardboard in those days. We would go around
the back of the A&P where the loading dock was.
There always were a few crates to get. One of the

great uses was to saw the corner off, nail a good rubber band, then stretch that and hook it up to the corner.

There was a linoleum store in the neighborhood. We would get scraps that were being thrown away, cut up linoleum into small squares, and place one between the stretched rubber band, then release. Those squares would sail like a Frisbee. It could do damage if it hit you. We got in trouble once in a while.

The parents in the neighborhood put a stop to that, so we would go to an empty lot to play cops and robbers. The empty lots were our territory. If we saw any of the parents coming, we took off quickly. Being chased was a rush. It was fun.

We were never bored. It was always either work or play.

Having a two-wheel bike was a big deal. Most of my friends had fancy bikes with lights and a horn. I kept bothering my father, telling him how important it was to have a bike. He always said we couldn't afford one, but promised that things were getting better and I would get one.

I finally got wise to how this could work. I told him I would use the bike to deliver orders, I would earn money with it. It worked!

It didn't take too long before he came home with good news. He found a used bike for five dollars advertised in the newspaper. We had to take the train to Prospect Park. It started to get dark. We got there, and I was so excited I could hardly stand still. It was a Mercury, had a light and a horn. I rode it to the corner to test it out. It was beautiful.

My father took the train home and I rode my bike the whole way.

The next day I couldn't wait to get home from school. The first place I went was the dry cleaner close by. I told him I would deliver cleaning. He thought that was a good idea. I would hold the handlebar with one hand and the hangers with clothes with the other.

I had to hold the hanger up high and the clothes would rest on my head. It was difficult at first, but I got used to it.

There were always some of the moms on the front steps knitting either a sweater, scarf or hat. Most of the time someone had a tray of fresh baked cookies. This was being raised by the village.

Good memories, for sure.

1939

I was going on seven years old. It was the first trip to King's County Hospital. Doctors were still trying to diagnose what was going on with my mom. My father could not afford to have someone come to our house to care of her.

I said goodbye when the ambulance came to take her. I was not allowed to visit. It was almost a year before we connected with a nurse who would sneak me up the backstairs.

My father wanted to do something to cheer me up. The thing was, everyone was checking to see how I was holding up. I was fine. At least, I thought I was.

One night my father gave me a choice. What would I rather have; a cowboy gun and holster; tickets for the circus at Madison Square Garden, or to go to the new Tarzan movie starring Johnny Weissmuller?

The first thought I had was, what did he think I would want? I didn't want to disappoint him.

I thought about asking my friends. The pressure was on.

The thing I really wanted was to go to the circus.

But, I thought he would think boys would want a holster and gun. So, to please him, I chose that.

Well, of course, he got tickets to the circus. I felt really bad. I told him I never want a gun. I really want to see the circus. I was convinced he didn't believe me.

That experience stayed with me for the rest of my life.

Six Years Old

Whenever we walked in the crowded city, my father held on to me by grabbing my wrist. It was really uncomfortable. So, I told him to hold my hand.

Once, when he was next to me, without thinking, I reached up and took his hand. We walked for a while and I looked up at a total stranger.

My father was angry, but not too angry to give me a learning experience.

The stranger that took my hand was not trying to steal me, he thought it was cute.

I was six years old. I wore knickers or short pants. When I switched to long pants, my mother was still in the hospital.

I was starting to see her once a week. She wanted to see me in my long pants. She had some advice for me. She said that when I sit down, pull my pants leg up. That way I would preserve the crease.

I know it sounds like a small thing, but I never forgot.

Herb Evans

Mother

In 1938 my mother was visiting my older sister in the hospital; she was being treated with a new treatment for polio, the Sister Kenny Treatment.

My mom told me to stay in the stroller with the groceries. There were other kids waiting outside also. Being distracted playing, a man grabbed a bag of food and took off.

When my mom came out and saw that the groceries were gone, she cried and yelled at me.

Still, in the Great Depression there were soup kitchens around the city. I felt like I failed, and this affected me for a long time.

I remember my mother, before she got sick, always working in the kitchen. Clothing was washed using a washboard, and then hung on a clothesline. In winter, my pants froze, they could stand by themselves. The alleys between the houses were always loaded with clothes hanging from the lines.

My mother had something wrong with her. She couldn't hold her head still. Doctors couldn't diagnose what it was, so they gave her a neck brace. After about a year they said it was multiple sclerosis, no cure, and no real treatment. It was getting worse.

My father couldn't afford to provide the care my mother needed. Finally, she went into the hospital. Kings County Hospital was huge. It was about four blocks long.

I was too young to be allowed to see her, so my father would take me on Sundays. A nurse would come down to a back door and let me sneak up the stairs, but only on Sunday, and only for a half hour. My mother was always happy to see me.

Mom was in a ward with 30 other women. They all needed constant care and couldn't afford home nurses. She always wanted me to walk around and say hello to everyone. She was in that ward for three years until she passed away.

During this time most of the moms in the neighborhood would invite me for supper.

After going to the hospital to visit, the smell of baked potatoes and medicine would come back to me out of nowhere, just walking down the street.

It was a few years where that would happen every day, then it started to become more once in a while. To this day, it still comes over me.

I'll never forget that day when my father came down and interrupted a game of punch ball. "We have to go," but it wasn't Sunday.

We took the trolley to East Flatbush in Brooklyn. He told me to wait across the street in front of a candy store. There were people coming in and out. I thought most of them were visiting people in the hospital. I was thinking of the punch ball game with my friends. I felt guilty, I just didn't want to be there.

It was 1944, I was ten years old, but I felt older. I was selfish; I wanted to be with my friends.

It was almost two hours, then I saw him coming across the street. He grabbed my arm and said, "We're going home." He didn't say anything and I didn't either.

We got on the trolley and finally he said "You know your mother is not coming home," and I just said, "I know."

I wanted to cry but I couldn't. I thought "now I can play with my friends", but I felt guilty. It was so strange, every time I visited, there was always a mattress folded over and I knew that person had died. Now I was thinking my mother's mattress must have been folded over.

My friends and their mothers came by the house to give their respects. The moms all gave me a hug and told me something wonderful about my mom. But still I couldn't cry.

It was about two years later, when out of nowhere as I was walking home from school I suddenly caught the odor of a dish she used to cooked that I liked.

I started to cry. I couldn't stop. My friends walking with me said, "What's wrong with you?" I said, "I'll see you later" and I ran ahead.

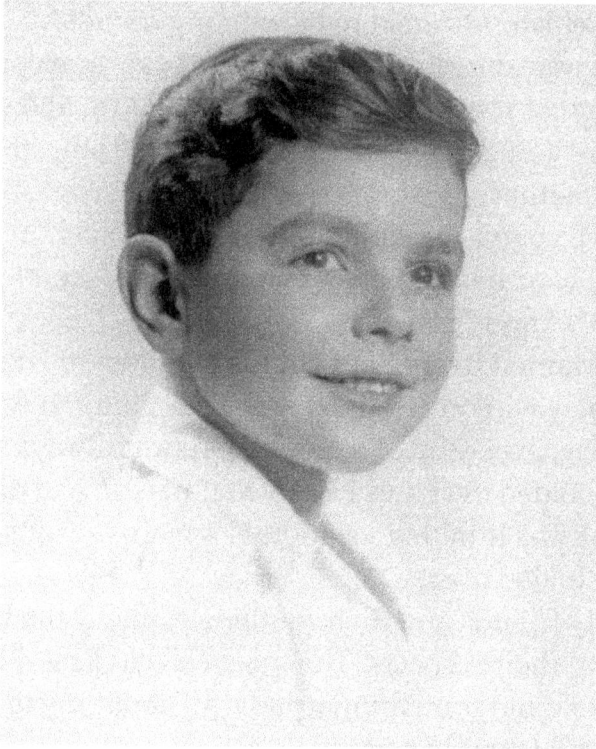

Herb Evans - 1939

1940's

Herb Evans

1945

Twelve years old - a plane crashed into the Empire State Building. It stayed sticking out of the seventy-ninth floor. I tried to get my friends to take the subway to Manhattan, Thirty Fourth Street and Sixth Avenue. At that point I could do anything I wanted. I had little patience with the rules that average twelve-year-olds had to live by. I wanted to see this!

When I got there, the streets were packed. The word was that the plane cut the elevator cables. People in the car went down seventy floors, free-falling.

There was a navy pharmacist in the crowd. He ran up seventy-nine floors a few times and saved lives. I thought "that's got to be a great thing, to be a hero." I was so glad I got to see this.

The next thing I saw on Fifth Avenue was a ticker-tape parade for Ike Eisenhower - a hero's welcome home from Europe. He had a smile that beamed down from the open limo. He waved at the crowd. It was magical.

These small events are like a window into my mother, my father, and me.

Jobs

I loved working. I wanted to see what this would look like if I could list all the jobs I had.

I started out creating my own because no one would hire me. I was too small and skinny. I went around the neighborhood and made it known that I was available for running errands, folding laundry, fixing clotheslines. I would get paid for any odd job, whatever they thought was fair, usually twenty-five cents.

After a while, I would hear my name being called when someone needed me. At the end of the day, I would sit on my bed and count the coins. I wasn't taken too seriously. Most of the neighbors thought it was cute.

My father gave me a bucket that I kept on the floor of the closet. After about a year I would sit on the stoop and wait for my first customer. It was getting known, if you needed something, get Herb. The stoop was my office. By the time I was almost nine years old, the bucket was almost full.

Herb Evans

The Phone

It started on the wall in the hall. It was shared by two apartments. It had its own personality. When it rang, everyone paid attention. My father was always amazed by it. When he spoke on it, his voice changed. He would practically yell into it. I was only eight and I knew you didn't have to yell. When I asked him about that, he would say "It's long distance. A few blocks and a joke away."

Then one day it came into the house on the wall in the kitchen. It was a party line, so if it rang and someone said "I got this", it was for another party. It was a puzzle – how can a voice, full words come through a telephone line? As time went on, it changed shape and it wasn't a party line any more. It didn't bother me. I took it any way as long as I could talk.

There were phone booths on the street, and for a nickel you could call someone. It was kind of funny, kids had no trouble with new phones, but old people were puzzled. Some kids found out how to get a dial tone without a nickel. The word spread fast from schoolyard to schoolyard. Pretty soon it was all over the city, but only for the kids. Simple! You stuck a pin in the line and then touched the pin to the coin box. It shorted and – viola! You made your call.

We didn't think that was stealing. We were cheating the phone. The phone company figured this out pretty quick, and they changed the line from rubber to corrugated steel. No more puncturing with a pin. Then we figured out how to use a washer the same size as a nickel – we called those slugs.

Then, suddenly phones came without a wire. Now that's scary. Phones came with buttons instead of dials, that took a little getting used to. Then the wildest thing – you could get a phone that had buttons on it that lit up when a call came in. It could be more than one call at a time. You could be talking and tell someone to hold on, and answer someone else who was calling you.

As time passed, phones got more complicated. Now, seventy years later, I have a phone in my pocket. I am just like my father, I really don't understand it. I am paying for the capability to perform magic, and I don't know how to use it. My son says, "Get on line, Dad," and I think of a circus performer.

I don't have a laptop, and I'm told I am backed up on the cloud. The image I get is a complete set of encyclopedias hanging from the Internet located inside of a cumulonimbus.

Movies

Movies became the most anticipated event every Saturday afternoon. The Dewey Theater would be packed. Most kids were around seven or eight, ten cents a ticket. There were at least two matrons controlling the kids.

When the movie was over, after the cartoon the first one hundred kids out would get a comic book. I would get too affected by the film, I never got a comic book, I just sat there until the matron would remind me I had to leave.

I remember a movie with James Cagney and Pat O'Brien, *Angels With Dirty Faces*. Cagney played a gangster and O'Brien played a priest. They were best friends as kids, doing petty thefts. Cagney gets caught and goes to reform school. When he gets out he pursues a life of crime, and Pat O'Brien becomes a priest.

The kids in the nieghborhood looked up to Cagney. He was a tough guy hero. In the end, he's convicted of murder and sentenced to the electric chair.

The priest meets with him and tells him, "It's important you go out kicking and screaming. The kids can't think you're a hero."

Cagney says he would never do that. But on his way, he breaks down, "I don't want to die," he cried. You never know if it was real or just an act for the kids.

There were lots of arguments about this. That's an example of living the film.

If I saw a swashbuckler with Douglas Fairbanks, Jr., for days after I would bounce around like an acrobat. When I saw *Young Man With A Horn* with Kirk Douglas, I felt the pain searching for that note that didn't exist. When I saw *Brute Force* with Burt Lancaster, I knew what it was like to be trapped in a federal prison.

I loved movies. Saturday afternoon it was what I did. I always had money doing odd jobs like delivering orders, hanging clotheslines, whatever they could get me. I used to go to the movies by myself only because I wanted to watch the film. Sometimes I took the subway to Times Square and hung out in front of a theater. At intermission, it was crowded outside with people taking a smoke. That's when you go in with the crowd. I saw some of the best Broadway shows at Saturday matinées (or half shows). Arthur Miller's *Death of a Salesman*. Lee J. Cobb was fantastic.

This Saturday afternoon activity was my little secret.

To Write is to Heal

The Japanese attacked Pearl Harbor. The war in Europe was in full swing. This was just before my mother was showing strange symptoms and the doctors could not come up with a diagnosis. She was not able to hold her head still. I was eight years old that summer.

They had to find something for me to do so they could deal with what was going on. My father found an organization called The Fresh Air Fund. I got to go to the country, hiking and learning to do all the things the Boy Scouts did.

When I played in the sun I got really dark fast. The counselor, Mel Marine, I think he was about sixteen, gave me the nickname "Blacky". I liked that, it made me feel special. Most of the boys were older teenagers. I had to put on my tough guy act, that's what worked best to protect me. It seems that most of my life I was protecting myself, on guard, a hell of a way to live.

As I got older, I perfected the act so it wasn't easy to detect. I also realized as I got older, it wasn't as dangerous as I imagined.

A Life of Crime

Our gang of boys were nine years old. One of the guys came up with the idea. At that time we were always wearing knickers, so this was brilliant. The pockets hung inside the pants, so, if you cut the bottom of the pocket and then, whatever you put in would fall down into the pant leg.

We would go into a Woolworth's Five and Dime Store and take turns browsing the magazine section. The rest of us would keep an eye out for the sales person. We would roll up comic books and slip them in our pockets. You would never think that a comic book would disappear into our small pockets.

When we walked out, each one of us had at least three books. Then, we would go to barber shops, ones that dealt with kids. We would get a nickel a piece for brand new comics. That would improve the shop's business.

One of the guys in our gang had a problem. His mom and dad thought it was time for him to start wearing long pants. That was a disaster.

He wanted to continue with us, by putting the books under his shirt. It was obvious, and he got busted.

It was over for us.

I was happy about it. I just went along because I wanted to be one of the guys. I made more money doing odd jobs. Our life of crime lasted one year. As far as I knew, everyone went straight.

You might say our crime spree was ended by long pants.

Being a Kid During the War

I was ten years old, the war in Europe and the Pacific was in full swing. The big guys, that's what we called eighteen-year olds, were all gone, drafted. The moms in the neighborhood would sit on the porch and ask the Ouija Board if their sons would come home. I didn't understand how that could work, but it was intense.

There were about four or five on each board, and a question was asked and the thing that was on the board would start sliding to different letters. It was strange, there were always screams and crying. I didn't think a game board like Ouija could tell you what was going to happen. But when you have a kid that's in harm's way, you can believe anything.

All I know is that there were blue stars in the windows that were being replaced by gold stars. I knew even at 10 years old that some of the big guys on the block would never come home. This was 74 years ago, but now I know what it felt like to have your son in harm's way. You grab at anything and make it possible.

My Father, A Russian Immigrant

The atom bomb was dropped on Hiroshima and Nagasaki, the Japanese surrendered. There were block parties with all kinds of food and cookies set up in the streets. People were laughing and crying. It was a confusing time for me. I couldn't understand how all this happened, some of my friends were wanting to drop another bomb on Japan. I was becoming more and more, what they called, a loner.

My father pulled me into the house. He wanted to talk – that was rare, and I remember it vividly. For the past four years, the propaganda was intense. The Japanese people were shown to be vicious, mean, and ugly. Every movie about the war was a propaganda tool.

My father was upset about the festive atmosphere. He explained the horror that just took place. "Yes, it's wonderful that the war was over, but you must respect all people." He was talking to me and only me. He was not the kind to preach to anyone.

I never forgot that. Now we are here, 2018, and discussing the fate of over a million immigrants, some don't know they are immigrants. I don't understand how it could be possible that these people can be deported to a strange land. I have regrets about not trying to understand the experiences that my father had as a young boy. It's easy to judge these people without knowing how it was growing up.

My father and I didn't have a lot of conversations. But it wasn't like he didn't want to talk, it was totally different for him in Russia. All through World War II, Russia was an ally, now it was different, there was paranoia and fear. I didn't understand completely what he was going through. One day a man came to our door and I never saw him so angry. They were recruiting for The Communist Party. He pushed the guy out and slammed the door shut. "Don't ever come back!" he yelled. He never spoke about it, but I knew there was fear on his face. I talked to a couple of friends. They were told not to discuss things like that. Some of the most talented people in the theatre were curious about socialism and slipped over the fine line to communism. Careers were destroyed and your name was on a blacklist.

I couldn't let go of the image of the parents, all immigrants. First growing up in that environment and then being in the service business for more than forty years, I didn't understand back then how scary it was. My father lived quietly under the radar. He and his brother had left Russia together, doing odd jobs and working on ships to get from one port to another. They were teenagers. The only reason I heard this story over time is because I pressed him. He was still frightened all those years that something could go wrong.

During their travels, they got separated. I don't know all the details, but somehow through the Red Cross, his brother was located in Argentina. It was now the late forties, after the war. He hadn't seen him for more than thirty years. They both had families and wrote letters. Finally, sometime in the 1960's, my father went to Argentina to meet his brother's family – a wife and four children. His brother never made it to America, but from what I understand had a full, successful life in Argentina.

In 1951 when I went into the Navy and volunteered for sub school, I had to fill out a questionnaire. They asked where my father was born, I was called back for more interviews. I can't be sure, but I felt like I was vetted more than the next guy. You had to be cleared for secrecy. We were lectured on the secrecy of speed, depth, acoustic torpedoes. The funny thing was that all that was published in Life Magazine.

I didn't know I was going to write about this and I felt a little resistance when I touched on my father, but it affected me, so there it is. I was a total American, an optimist, I thought. I had my opportunity, could go and live anywhere. No boundaries for me, but for him, he was a foreigner, caught in the middle. How do you raise a kid? The values that he had to live by were totally oppressive to me. I didn't have anybody to talk to about it.

One time he took me for a walk on the boardwalk on Coney Island, a rare event. He wanted to connect. I felt all that he was feeling without a word being spoken. As we walked, we passed a group of men, they acknowledged my father. As we passed them he said, "They haven't any family. Family is the most important." I never forgot that. We walked on in silence.

He finally said, "I met a woman, I have been seeing her for a while. What do you think about that?" I was almost fourteen years old. I felt totally independent of him. I told him that was good, it must be lonely after my mom passed away. That was all that was said.

I moved into a friend's apartment and was able to contribute to expenses.

Sy was like a brother to me. His mom was a loving person to the whole neighborhood. The apartment was over a small grocery store. The building was overrun with mice. Sometimes we would be sitting on the couch listening to the radio and a mouse would run across the floor right in front of us. Nobody seemed to care. Mrs. Schlossman would just shoo it away.

I shared the room with Sy until we started high

school, then I moved out and got a room of my own.

My father married his new partner. She was a school teacher with two daughters, a real disciplinarian. They lived in Brooklyn in a section called East New York. When she met me, the first thing she said was, "Stay away from my daughters." I couldn't believe it. I never mentioned that to my father, but I was glad I was out of there.

Now, on with my life.

A Dream That He Wanted

To be a part of
To belong with
To give to
To create comfort
To welcome in
To share food
To share health
To be an immigrant
To be...

Herb Evans

A Leap of Faith

I remember when I was twelve years old and atomic bombs were dropped on Hiroshima and Nagasaki. I thought that I would never live to see twenty. Imagine, twelve years old and having no faith.

My mother had died and my sister left home. I was already thinking about getting a room somewhere. It took me another two years to take that leap. I was going to James Madison High School, so I stayed in the same neighborhood, same friends, and being raised by the village.

I don't want to give the impression that I wasn't enjoying my life. I was taking care of myself and I laughed a lot. I kept my dark thoughts to myself. I always had money to do what I wanted, working after school every day, mostly having dinner at one of my friend's houses. Life was pretty good. I tried to keep it light.

The next important leap was high school graduation.

My friends and their parents were in stress of what to do now. Some were going to college, some were going to work for their fathers. I was in observation mode.

This is getting serious, I am just turning eigh-teen, it looks like I will make it to twenty. I'd better make a move. This is going to be the biggest leap yet. I'm no longer this cute kid appearing to run wild on the streets. Of course, I felt I had it under control. It seems like the leap to being a responsible adult was so sudden, it was jarring.

Being a dad and then a granddad, I know it's a cliché to say that time flies, but this life has been one hell of a "leap of faith."

Different Families, Different Food

I felt lucky. I saw all the moms on the block like a menu. I know this sounds terrible, but if I felt like Italian, I would go over to Joey's mom, Mrs. Sangimeno; Sy's mom Mrs. Schlossman made the best meatloaf; Mrs. Goldberg made the best casserole dishes. Most things in my life seemed comical to me.

There was lots of laughter around the family tables of my friends. Even though it seemed like my childhood was rough, I was counting my blessings. My father always treated me with respect and valued my opinions.

Twelve years old and dreaming about some time living in the country. My mother had passed away, my sister was leaving home. My father was working mostly. I spent lots of time with different families on the block. I had secrets from my friends, things I did on my own, mostly I didn't want to share my thoughts. Don't get me wrong, I had good friends. We had fun together, but I had secrets.

I worked a lot, so I always had more money, so I could do things like go to the city and sneak into a show at intermission. I liked to take the bus to the Cloisters. It was like another world, built by the Rockefellers, stone by stone it was shipped over and put together like it was. I could sit there for hours and listen to the Gregorian Chants. I felt that my friends would think this was weird. I could have been wrong about that, but it's what I thought.

The bus ride up Madison Avenue was a show in itself. You got through some pretty rough neighborhoods. The Cloisters was the last stop on the Hudson River. It took me out of East Twenty Fourth in Brooklyn to another time. On the way up, I saw fights over a seat, heated arguments over a baseball game, people yelling at one another, then I got off at the Cloisters. Quiet, peaceful, beautiful.

Exploring

When I was 15 years old, I got a job in a radio repair shop installing TVs. A short-lived job, but all my jobs were short-lived. My boss, Eddie Ames, could repair anything.

I thought the console radios, before transistors, were miracles. For a moment I thought maybe I could learn, and this could be a career. That idea lasted a little more than a day. Eddie said the opportunity was to install TVs.

We would carry the TVs into the house, run a wire up to the roof, mount the antenna to the chimney. I would have earphones on, Eddie would be telling me which way to rotate the antenna. I was the guy on the roof, no matter what the weather. If the roof was an A-Frame and it was freezing, I would be sliding all over the place. There definitely was no future in my mind, better to go from job to job.

I was always better off creating my own way of earning money. I was pretty sure of myself, but it was always a leap to get the boss to have confidence in certain jobs because I looked too young.

I was already leaning towards joining the Navy. That was my own secret. After graduating high school and going through a few more jobs, I bit the bullet and joined up.

Herb Evans

A Memory

A balmy summer night, hanging with the guys in front of the corner candy store. A luxury is to get an egg cream. That's a specialty known only in Brooklyn. It doesn't have egg or cream, just chocolate syrup, a touch of milk, and seltzer. The soda water comes out of the spigot at high speed and causes the drink to foam up. Now, THAT's an egg cream!

We are all just standing around eating peanuts and spitting the shells on the sidewalk. The conversation is, "What do you want to do tonight?" That's answered with, "I don't know, what do you want to do?" Then back and forth, "let's shoot pool," or, "how about bowling." It's really tough to get these guys off the corner. I would get restless and start to pull away and go off on my own. They would complain, "There you go, always in a hurry."

Well, this time I didn't go fast enough. Jack Stanton pulls up in a beautiful convertible Lincoln, the longest car I ever saw.

"C'mon, let's go for a ride out to the beach. My uncle came to visit and said I could use it." We all piled in. Another few minutes and I would have already been gone.

We're sailing down the belt parkway, the breeze feels so good. I was getting comfortable when, you guessed it, flashing lights. We pull over and are ordered to line up on the side of the highway. There are two patrol cars and four cops. I'm wondering what's going on.

Okay, Jack doesn't have a license. Not the end of the world. We are waiting, seemed like a long time. Finally, a paddy wagon pulls up and we are ordered to get in. "You guys are going to jail. Hope this will teach you not to go joyriding in a stolen car." Jack, are you crazy? Seventy years ago, this was getting complicated. Back then, if you were under eighteen, your legal guardian took the rap for whatever you did.

The parents were showing up. It was not a mellow scene. It was loud, and different languages were being yelled. It was crazy. Jack confessed that he took the car and we had nothing to do with it. The truth is that it was his uncle's car, but he didn't ask for permission.

I didn't want to call my father, this was more than he could handle. Lucky for me one of the guys had a really cool dad and he claimed me, so I went home with them. The experience that most immigrants had in the old country, as they called it, was not good. That's why they're here, where it was supposed to be better.

It's 2018 and all I hear about immigration is deportation, and it brought me back to this incident. Are we ever going to change? Most of the neighborhood was working on their citizenship. They were petrified to come to a jail, not because they did anything, but because of their experience in the past. My father told me how the Cossacks would ride into a village on horseback and tell everyone to move out. They ask why? Because the czar said so. Next step, go to America...

Last week, in my writing group I was reading about this incident I had with my friends, and it brought to mind the fear that our parents as immigrants were living with. In the middle of reading, I couldn't focus on the words and Tom was kind enough to finish it. I spent that night in Community Hospital, where they had me hooked up with all sorts of wires and an IV to hydrate me. It's impossible to sleep with nurses coming in to check on you every couple of hours. I passed my physical, of course. They checked everything except my eyes. I made an appointment to see an ophthalmologist.

Tom stopped by the next day to see how I was doing. That lifted my spirits. I was getting released and feeling good, but aware that I had to make sure I had enough electrolytes and water.

Herb Evans

Pool

I discovered the life of a pool shooter. I turned sixteen and now was allowed in. There was a place that had bowling alleys, and us kids would set pins. You had to be able to hold four pins at a time and set them on the spots. This is before the automatic machines. Speed was important. You had to lift yourself up high so you wouldn't get hit by any flying pins. There were some really good bowlers that had their special kids to set for them, especially if there was money on the line.

The pool tables were on the other side of the room. It was a gambling room, quiet and intense around the tables. These guys were serious. You'd better not move if a player was stroking a stick. Run your hand over the green and you can tell if it is tight. A good stretched green would let the balls roll easily. Bounce the cue ball off the rail to see how alive the table is. You're playing the table as much as your opponent. I guess I could have spent my time more productively.

From the time I turned 16, my time was spent with school, work, and then at 6:00, down to the pool room. If my friends wanted to find me, they knew where I would be.

Those two years before I went into the navy, I considered an important learning experience. I spent more time watching the action on the tables than playing.

I got really good at sizing up the odds on a game. Everything was considered – the way a guy would pick up a cue stick, how he would feel the table, how smooth and steady his stroke was, the control of the cue ball to get in position for the next shot. I never wanted to play if it wasn't serious. That's why I rarely shot pool with my friends. It was no fun if there wasn't any money on it.

High School, Graduation

When I was 14 years old and started James Madison High School. I had special working hours, no extra curricula like study period or lunch. I went from 8 a.m. to 12:00, then I had a few jobs, mostly as delivery boy. There were 8,000 students, most classrooms had forty kids. One of my classes was over-full. I stood at the window using the sill as my desk. I always passed my classes, but not by much.

Making money after school was much more interesting to me. I only remember one teacher the whole 4 years of high school, an English teacher, Dr. Sarota, who showed an interest. Years later when I opened my first restaurant, he came by to see how I was doing.

Getting close to graduation, in 1950, I realized I'd better pay attention at school. We had to take regent exams and I definitely wanted a diploma. I went to see my father about it. He was not too excited about higher education. He always said learn a trade, that was more secure. I didn't really understand what his experience was as a kid, but he had trouble trusting. I would tell him, "Don't worry, I can always create income." I was optimistic, and he was the opposite.

Our graduation class was so big that we had to have the ceremony at the Brooklyn Paramount, a large theater. No giving out diplomas, we were told to come back in a week and pick them up. We had a couple of songs to sing and some speeches and were told to make sure we were registered for the draft.

I was seated with what they called the listeners. Our music teacher told us to mouth the song. She said we would ruin the performance. Can you imagine mouthing the Italian street song, *Zing, Zing, Zing, Zing Boom Boom A Madelanies Gay* That was not a good music teacher. I think she ruined my singing career.

After this was over, I went to one of my friend's houses for a celebration. His family was all saying goodbye, most of the kids were going to college. My friend's dad cornered me and tried to talk me into working for him. I finally excused myself and thanked them.

When I graduated the beginning of 1951, most of my friends were on a clear path, either school or working for their fathers. The Korean War was on and the draft was in effect. I thought, if I don't do something I could end up in a muddy foxhole.

I went in to the recruiting office for the Navy. I signed up for eight years, four active and four reserves. I was eighteen years old. I took a test, a "G.C.T.", General Classification. They offered me a wide variety of choices. I chose to work on engines. They sent me to New London, Connecticut, to a submarine tender. That was a big ship that repaired and serviced submarines.

I knew immediately I wanted submarine duty. I went to the officer in charge and made my case. My grade on the G.C.T. was high, and after a series of physical exams, I was accepted to sub school.

1950's

Herb Evans

Eighteen Years Old

I just graduated James Madison High School. It was a hot June day and I was thinking about what was next. Republic Aviation in Farmingdale, Long Island, was looking for employees. They were paying pretty good wages, $1.65 an hour.

A friend of mine, Tommy Maziotti, and I went out to the plant, figuring we would work the whole summer, save some money, and that would give us time to figure it out.

We both got hired and were told to come back the next day. To get out there was not easy. Tommy borrowed a car that first day. It was such a piece of junk, I didn't think it would make it. Gas was 25 cents a gallon, we had to return the car. So we made a sign that said, "Republic Aviation" and went out on the Belt Parkway, 6:30 in the morning.

Cars were racing past, but it wasn't too long before we got a ride. The guy was going to the plant. It seemed that most of the cars were going to Republic. He wanted a fifty-cent appeasement that would help with the gas. He would pick us up every day. That first day was really interesting, the plant was manufacturing F-84 Thunderjets.

We went to a class, it was set up like school. We were told how important the work would be. These were the main fighting jets that were used in Korea. Tommy and I were not interested in politics, I didn't even know why we were fighting, all I knew was, we were the good guys and they were the bad guys.

This started to change for me. I didn't trust the propaganda. I mean, the movies and the newsreels, how can the enemy all look evil? I thought John Wayne was a joke. My friends started to criticize me. After the summer I decided to get out of Brooklyn. I was fine to go it alone. Most of my friends were on a path that was chosen for them.

I took the subway up to the City, that's what we called Manhattan. Walking down Broadway there were recruiting stations in storefronts, Army, Navy, Air Force, Coast Guard. I was interested in the Navy since I was a little kid, hanging out at the navy base in Brooklyn, Sheepshead Bay. I was walking along thinking of the short time I spent at Republic Aviation. It was a good experience, they had me inspecting the planes at the final station. I had a mirror on a long rod and a flashlight. Those were all the tools I had. I was looking at all the rivets to see if any were loose. There was a serious accident.

At lunch break, a guy was eating his sandwich sitting in the cockpit when the catapult went off. He went flying, maybe twenty feet in the air. They cleared us out pretty quick. I heard the guy was killed. My thoughts were fixed on how fragile and unknown life is. I was very serious back in those days. Now I was on Broadway in front of the Navy recruiting station.

I sat down on a bench. It seemed like I sat there for a long time. There were so many thoughts in my mind, my head was hurting. I went in and was interviewed. They were really nice, and I started to relax. I felt good. I signed up for eight years. I didn't have to think about what I was going to do. It was all laid out for me.

Submarine School

At eighteen years old I was accepted to submarine school in New London, Connecticut. It's all voluntary, so there was about fifty per cent of the class dropping out.

Escape procedures was the experience that I remember most, maybe because it was really doing it. You get into a pressure compartment on the ground. There's a tower attached to it, it's one hundred feet high filled with water. At one hundred feet the pressure at the bottom is sixty pounds per square inch. This is going to be a free ascent.

A chief diver is with us, he's a tough old guy. He looks like most of his experience lies is in the water, the rest is in alcohol. He opens the hatch to the chamber and five of us step in. He then slams it closed and spins the wheel and makes it water-tight. The five of us are seated on a bench. He did this so fast and smooth. I thought this may be the end of my life. It's crazy, but the first thing that popped into my head was that I never had a steady girlfriend.

Now he said, "Listen carefully, I'm going to bleed air in until the pressure is equal to the water. Just breathe normally. If anyone wants out, just raise your hand. That's the only way out. The next step is you going up. I'm going to open the valve now."

The noise of the air coming in was enough to scare the hell out of you. Three hands went up immediately. He turned the air off and opened the hatch, the three left, I never saw them again. I guess that was the end of their training.

Now there were just the two of us with the chief. The chief dogged the hatchback and opened the air. I was sitting on my hands, that was the only way I kept them from flying up. The air pressure was up and my heart was pounding.

The chief said, "Now listen, this is vital to your survival. I'm going to open this other hatch and you're going to step into this wall of water, the pressure is equal so the water won't rush in. Now it's natural to want to hold your breath, but you have all that air pressure in your lungs and they're porous, so air will push through and send a bubble to your heart. That's air embolism. You will whistle Dixie and keep releasing air. If you don't, you will die.

If you go faster than the bubbles, the pressure on your body will be reduced too fast as you go up, and you can get the bends. In that case, we will throw you in a decompression chamber and we will bring you back and slowly release the pressure. You won't die, but it can be painful."

Well, here we go. Strange to step into a wall of

water. At one point I started to go faster than the bubbles, but the chief slowed me down. When we got to the surface, I felt great, the chief said we did good, you're still alive. That's all there is. That was the finish of the month of school.

I was to leave the next day to Key West, Florida, to report to the *Sea Cat*, a fleet-type sub converted to a snorkel. It takes about six months before you qualify for your dolphins. There's one other type of escape to go through, that's the diving bell, and that is in the open ocean.

This is not high tech, take a glass and press a paper towel into it. Face the open end of the glass down, and submerge it, then bring it up. The towel will be totally dry. The air trapped in the glass prevents the water from going up. That's exactly what we did with the bell, except the dry towels are us.

On the *Sea Cat*, I became the movie operator if we were going out for an extended mission. I selected the films, always with characters that I could relate to. The guys complained, but nobody else wanted the job. I felt a lot happier than I seemed. I had a need, a flair for the dramatic. Looking back at nineteen, I was always living a role from one of the films. The guys would tease me, good-natured, like, "Okay, Herb, who are you today?"

Learning on a Sub

I was in a barracks with about 100 other guys. Sub duty was a special service. After two months there were less than half of us left. Most dropped out after the underwater escape tests. I was assigned to the *USS Sea Cat SS399* in Key West, Florida. School on the boat went on for almost a year. You had to know every nut, bolt, and screw. It took a year of study before you could wear your dolphins. Now you're qualified. It's like getting your wings.

I liked the engine room, no one wanted to be there. This gave me plenty of time to dream about what I wanted when I got out. I thought of staying in for twenty years, a good retirement if I lived through it.

A full complement of officers and crew was eighty. We only had forty. It was hard to get full crews. We would have to stand watch four hours on and four off. That meant only three and a half hours' sleep.

Most times we would dive to 500 feet and practice avoiding the destroyer and other surface craft that were searching for us. Subs were electric boats;

we had 120 tons of batteries. When we had to charge them, we would come up to 50 feet and raise a snorkel mast and turn on the engines. These were 1600 horsepower diesel engines.

This was a tricky procedure because if the sea was rough, the snorkel would shut down if a wave came over, then we had to manually shut the engines. It never occurred to me that this was a dangerous job. When you're nineteen years old, you think you're invincible.

My last year, in 1955, a sub went on a deep dive and didn't come up. Fifty of the crew were lost. I thought, wouldn't it be ironic after all this time if that happened to the *Sea Cat*? That's the first time I thought about it. I didn't dwell on it, but I became more aware of the possibilities. November 1955, my release was coming up. Twenty-two years old and now I would run my own life, little things like what to wear, what to eat, where to live, things that I took for granted for the last four years.

Funny thing, the navy always used their recruiting slogan "Join the Navy and see the world". Well, there are no windows in subs, and its mostly secret missions, so you don't see anything. But it was a wonderful experience for me.

On the Sub

Cruising at 500 feet on the *USS Sea Cat 399*, it's funny, whenever I mention my sub I have to state the whole name and number. I was well trained, I was surprised to find that I liked to follow orders, I enjoyed not having to decide what my life was going to be like.

Most of the time I didn't even know what our mission was, we were just the kids. The older guys, the chiefs, and rated men were in charge. I was an engine man. My job was to do as I was told. When we were submerged, our power was batteries. The engines were only used on the surface or when we had to charge the batteries. We could do that snorkeling at fifty feet.

I was the youngest, only eighteen when I came on board. My boss, Jody Taylor, was a First Class Petty Officer, he had four hash marks. Each one represented four years – sixteen years in the engine room. He knew his job, and he was teaching me. I wanted to do a really good job. He couldn't have been a better boss.

He advised me about getting along with the rest

of the crew. I asked him why that would be an issue. I never had a problem getting along. Well, I was surprised. It seems that the first day I reported, I dropped my duffel bag down the hatch. It had in big letters, Brooklyn, New York. Before I even got down the ladder, the guys had an opinion, and it was going to be uphill from there. Most of the crew were either from Texas, Louisiana, or Florida, anywhere but Brooklyn.

I told Jody, don't worry, I can take care of myself. Well, he said, that's the attitude that will get you in the most trouble. I learned a lot more than engines. How lucky to have a man like Jody looking out for me. He was a man of minimum conversation, but I listened and I got it. I think he was one of the most important teachers I ever had. It blows my mind that this was sixty five years ago and it's as clear as yesterday.

It feels good to acknowledge Jody Taylor.

War Games

We were part of a wolf pack, that's about six submarines covering a given area. Surface craft destroyers and destroyer escorts were trying to find us. One of the most popular games, when I was a kid, was hide and seek, only this was serious. They were armed with depth charges and hedgehogs. The explosions were not full strength, but enough to let you know you've been hit.

The depth charges were set to explode at a certain depth. The explosion was strong enough to shake you up. The hedgehogs were like hand grenades. They would throw a cluster of them – they were counter-mined so if one hit and exploded, they all went off.

I knew that this was a game, but it felt real, and I kept thinking, could they make a mistake? It got crazy.

I was in the engine room. We were running on batteries, so I didn't have much to do. The executive officer decided to come up to periscope depth and take a look.

This might be a mistake I thought. The minute

that scope popped up and the officer of the deck looked out, he gave the order "Dive! Dive!" A destroyer was barreling right towards us. Before we could get deep enough, the scope got hit. We came close to rolling over, which could have been an explosion and the end.

This was serious.

The scope was a new T.D.C., Torpedo Data Computer, the kind that when it gets the target, it gives you the information you need to fire a torpedo. The cost of one of these periscopes, more than a million dollars. That's 1952 dollars. The game was over for us and the destroyer that hit us.

This was a mistake that was going to end some careers. Lucky it didn't end some lives. The investigation and repair took a couple of months. I was able to have some great down-time in Myrtle Beach.

My boss, Jody Taylor, told me for sure we'd be going to Charleston, South Carolina Navy Yard.

When we put out to sea, we had a new skipper and new executive officer. There were a few of our crew that got on land and just quit. One of the guys said, "I've had it, that was the stupidest thing I ever saw."

I wonder why I'm telling this story sixty-five years later. I wonder how, at this point in my life, I'm still here. I have six children, including two sons-in-law and one daughter-in-law, seven grandchildren, three boys and four girls, some ex-wives and ex-girlfriends. But most importantly, all still friends.

My father was an atheist. I had no introduction to the belief in a God. So even with this close call, I had a plan, and I was convinced I would survive. Of course, when you're nineteen, it's easier to think like that.

Through the years there were instances where I was exposed to what I called the believers. It wasn't that I voiced an opinion or judged people, it was just that I didn't know and I didn't give it any thought.

I seemed to sail through life and go wherever the current took me. When I think of the forties, fifties, sixties, seventies, every decade I was part of the pulse of what was happening. It was the start, in the beginning, not feeling that I had a direction. Maybe that's what my smart kids picked up on, that's what kept pushing me to this room.

I was thinking that I'm through with this memoir, but no – I was just scratching the surface, covering up real feelings with theatrical stories. It takes more courage to expose who you really are than all the years under water.

Herb Evans

R & R in Cuba

I was entering the harbor in Havana, Cuba, nineteen years old. I had little knowledge of the world around me. Havana was a playground and a money machine for the Mafia.

Being an engineer, I was below deck sitting between two 1600-horsepower diesel engines. We called them rock crushers. It was hot, but the worst part was the noise. It's amazing that I can still hear!

I thought to myself, don't complain. I asked for this job because no one would come into the engine room unless they had to. I was always protecting myself, that was ingrained in my thinking from the streets of Brooklyn.

My sub was stationed in Key West, Florida, only ninety miles from Cuba, closer to Havana than the mainland of the U.S. I was feeling the excitement – we were pulling in to tie up. The captain announced over the sound system to meet in the after battery for instructions.

The Executive Officer made it very clear: listen to what he had to say, this is serious! Number One, don't talk politics. Number Two, under no circumstances do you pick up a girl on the street. If you go

Herb Evans

somewhere with this innocent young girl, we may not see you again. If you want to meet a girl, the Navy has pro stations set up, so you check in and they will direct you to a safe house. These girls were registered, and the way the Navy had control, you might say the Navy was acting like a pimp!

I was the movie-goer, the romantic. I couldn't see the romance in this arrangement.

The Number One, politics, that was more dangerous. The head of government was Batista. There were uniformed soldiers with rifles and sidearms on every block. There was talk about this guy Castro up in the mountains. He and his buddy Che Guevara were causing some problems.

My shipmate and I walked into a casino much like Las Vegas. Definitely mobbed up. We thought with these wise guys and the soldiers in the street, Castro and his buddy Che don't stand a chance.

Like I said, I had little world knowledge, but neither did the U.S. The opinion the United States had was even if the rebels drove Batista out, they would only last a couple of months. Well, fifty years later, we're thinking maybe we should be friendly with the still-in-charge Castro.

Another fiasco was the invasion of the Bay of Pigs in 1961. The CIA put together a group of exiles to take back the country, totally underestimating the security and armed forces that Castro had. Arrogance is a dangerous attitude.

Key West, Florida

Seems like a regular job, we had barracks to sleep in. Get up at 5:30 in the morning, walk down to the boat, have breakfast, and get ready to put out to sea.

They call this "daily operations".

We'd be part of training for war, there would be surface craft participating. I never knew what the game was, but the orders would come over the sound system. When we got to the area, the first thing I heard was, "Dive! Dive! Dive!", immediately shut down the engines. We were at a dive angle, you had to hold on or you would fall forward.

Over the loudspeaker, "The smoking light is out."

That's because now we are being powered by batteries, 126 cells of dry acid, each cell weighs one ton, it throws off chlorine gas enough to cause a fire. Hence, no smoking.

We would level off at 500 feet, surface craft are trying to find us. Depth charges were dropped, not loaded, but if you got hit, it was loud. Over the speaker, "Rig for depth charge."

This is all done manually, no high tech here.

We have a heavy steel hatch that is lifted and bolted under the existing hatch. There's one in the after-engine room where I am. So it's me and my partner. Neither one of us are big, and lifting that inner hatch was a struggle. If a depth charge explodes, even if it wasn't a hit, it could blow the upper hatch, so we have the inner to back us up. A depth charge is like a barrel and is pushed off a surface ship. You can hear them over our heads. We have to be quiet, sound travels in water clearly. I was living the movie *Run Silent, Run Deep*. I was Burt Lancaster today, so I was safe. You can't hurt Burt Lancaster.

This is going to sound so strange I didn't share it beyond my engine room. There was a small publication that would come out once a month called Ripley's, *Believe It Or Not*.

When the Holland Tunnel was being constructed under the Hudson River, the guys were called Sand Hogs.

A caisson would be lowered. It was basically a huge pipe open on both ends, about 30 feet in diameter. After it was on the bottom, the water would be pumped out. The crew of sandhogs then would go down and build the tunnel thirty feet at a time.

Ripley had a story that, one time when the guys were working, the caisson tilted slightly and one of the guys got sucked under in a bubble. He shot to the surface and landed on the deck of a barge. If that's not crazy, I don't know what is.

But I thought it could be possible. We had a 3,000-pound air system in the engine compartment, and I figured if we were in an emergency situation, I could dog the compartment hatches down and start bleeding air in, building up pressure, get up to the hatch and undog it, stay crouched next to it. When the pressure built up to the water, the hatch would fly open and I would go up in a bubble. That's the way I lived my life, always in possibility.

I never found out if that Ripley story was true, but who cared? The possibility was enough for me.

Key West was the last of the Florida Keys, two miles by one. Duval Street was two miles. There were one hundred bars and clubs, mostly playing country music. You had to be twenty-one to drink or even be in some of the places.

There were twelve thousand sailors on this base. The odds of meeting a girl were slim or impossible, especially if you weren't twenty-one. So mostly I stayed on the base, but if you wanted to take a chance and sneak in, there were a few that let you pass. The shore patrol would be checking IDs up and down Duval Street, so most of the time I played it safe.

The daily operations were getting more intense. We were diving deep and the pressure was causing leaks around the valves. One time we went out and were snorkeling, running the engines, diving and coming back to fifty feet and snorkeling. We did that for thirty days. It was hot and oily, no showers. We had a still in the forward engine room to make enough fresh water to wash your face and brush your teeth.

There were rumors that Castro and his right-hand, Che Guevara, were in the mountains getting ready to overthrow Batista. Batista was the dictator backed by the U.S. and controlled by the mafia.

We would go to Havana for R&R. There were gambling casinos, no age restrictions, it was a play-ground. The only thing we were warned about: Don't mention anything about politics. There were a few cases where some guys got drunk and were talking about Castro and Che. They were locked up, and one of them was in jail more than a year.

We were told our government would not help us if we got in trouble. Back at home, I was get-ting stir-crazy. I decided to go out one evening and walked to the southernmost bar in the country, "The Casa Marina". This is a cocktail bar in the hotel, the classiest place on the strip. I sat down at the bar and the barmaid, that's what women bartenders were called, she was pretty and had a friendly smile, asked for my ID, and of course, I was almost twen-ty-one, but not yet. She said she was sorry, but I could sit at a table and get a coke.

I felt like Holden Caulfield in *Catcher in the Rye*, almost a man, but not quite. When she took her break, I was surprised that she came over and sat with me. She became a friend. I stayed nursing a coke till 2:00 a.m., I talked to her on two different breaks. This was the best time I ever had going out in Key West.

I didn't get much sleep, but when you're twenty, who needs sleep?

Herb Evans

Maneuvers in the Caribbean

While on maneuvers in the Caribbean, we pulled into Port Au Prince in Haiti. We had a couple of days to be tourists. I visited a factory that manufactured bowls made out of beautiful teak and mahogany.

I remember flirting with a beautiful girl at the front desk. She said she was the owner's daughter. They were from Syria, seemed like a great family. The dad invited me to their home and to stay for dinner.

The home was beautiful, up on a hill overlooking the sea. It was rare to spend time with a family in these ports. There was a reason that the Navy had a bad reputation – drunken sailors.

They hit the first bar and never got out of the waterfront joints. If you wanted to bond with the old salts, as they were called, you got drunk with them. But when you were out at sea you'd better do your job, the entire sub depended on you.

Memories of Sub and Smitty

I have been struggling this week. All kinds of stories have been flowing in my brain, it was giving me a headache.

One incident that I didn't want to think about, but which kept popping up no matter what: My best friend Smitty on the *Sea Cat*. He came from the south, a black family, impoverished. Smitty was smarter than anyone I knew.

He wanted to be a radio operator, but the Navy back then was segregated. He was assigned to the captain and the executive officer as a steward's mate. He slept in a small compartment in the forward battery. He was responsible for the officers' shoes and uniforms.

We are all in nine sections of sewer pipe, that's what we called our sub. If we went down, we all went together. It was hard to believe that segregation was accepted as a normal thing and wasn't even talked about.

One time we were tied up for a break in Key West, so the crew wanted to have a ship's party. Everyone chipped in and we rented a hall and set up a bar, hired the music, decorated. It was festive and exciting.

Smitty came to me and said he was told he couldn't attend. The hotel that the hall was in wouldn't allow Negroes, that's what they were called back then. I was more upset than he was. Smitty was calming me down. He was totally okay with this. I mean, that was life, how it always was for him.

I didn't go to the party. We stayed on board, played chess, then watched a movie, then talked a lot about how illogical the rules were. I always knew about prejudices, but this was the first time it was up close and personal. Things were slowly opening up about segregation, and Smitty was pushing to take the exam for Radioman. Normally you would go to school, but the best he could do was get the books and study on his own.

He finally got to take the exam, and like I said, he was the smartest guy I knew. He got such a high grade, there was no stopping him. It took time, but he got rated as a Radioman. This was the start of breaking down the barriers. It was happening on ships and bases all over the Navy.

Smitty got transferred to another sub. I didn't see much of him after that. You could be as close as brothers, but transferred to another ship or base and you were gone.

Yes, there is a Santa Claus

I was just released from the Navy and working as a Christmas helper in Macy's Department. Store. My friend Bob and I were assigned to the women's ice skate department. You couldn't possibly take two twenty-two-year-old guys and put them in a better place. Yes, there IS a Santa Claus.

Herb Evans

Christmas at The Floral Studios

There weren't any flowers, not even a photo of one. The halls and the rooms were a dark green. The lighting was bare bulbs hanging down the center of the hallway. The floor was clean linoleum. Every ten feet was a standing ashtray. Pretty dismal, but I must admit it was clean. The odor of Pine Sol hung in the air.

I started to design the place in my head; a few simple change, bright colors, frosted bulbs to soften the lighting. I could almost see the changes. We have power in our thoughts.

Bob, the friend I met in line outside of Macy's was living with his mom in Brooklyn. He invited me to Christmas dinner. I picked up a box of assorted cookies. My father told me, "Never arrive empty handed."

Francis, his mom, talked loud and seemed tough, but really wasn't. It's a New York thing. You couldn't get any sympathy from her. She would hear us complain about some silly thing at work and she'd say, "Listen you guys, you're still on your way in. I'm on my way out." She said, "Wait another thirty years."

There was always a slight smile hidden at the corner of her mouth.

After dinner I had to catch the subway back to the Floral Studios. I was almost feeling a little depressed. There weren't a lot of people on the train, but the ones that were there didn't look that merry.

I got to my room and lay flat on my back, staring at the ceiling. Suddenly, a black spider came out of a crack in the ceiling where the wire holding the bare bulb hung. I was fascinated to see that walking across the ceiling upside down.

Does it know it looked like a vast desert. Then it let a line come down, or was it going up?

That slight depressed feeling was gone. I was not alone. Not everyone has a Merry Christmas. It can be painful for some. I had a job, a place to live, some money in my pocket. Everything seemed so temporary. For the next few days I kept seeing the spider, going in and out. I wondered what was it like inside that crack. I didn't know much about spiders, but it seemed that it had purpose, intelligence.

It made its way across the ceiling to the corner. It started to build a web. I watched for a while, and then fell asleep.

When I woke up, the web was finished. It was beautiful and intricate. The spider was gone. I know this sounds crazy, but, if you can be thankful for a spider, you can always find something to be grateful for.

I was still trying to get used to being out of the Navy. My mind drifted to the family that I lived with underwater for four years. Did I do the right thing? Getting out I mean. I felt that was the closest family I ever had. I thought that if I couldn't adjust, I would sign up again. I had four more years in the reserves. I was safe for the time being.

Monday rolled around and we had another week in Macy's. Bob was totally OK being out of the Air Force. It was different for him. I was always coming from survival, where ever I was. Acting class, restaurant work, no matter what, I had one foot in and one foot out. I was always ready for escape.

It seemed like that was a pattern I developed for the rest of my life. I was considered successful. I built seventeen different businesses with one foot in and one foot out. There was always a spider around somewhere, building a complicated web.

Herb Evans

Shake it Don't Break It

I was feeling like I got to get out. I went down and out on Eighth Avenue. There was always lots of people on the street. Usually I was Okay in my room, but this night I felt I was losing it.

As usual the hustlers were out in force. One con was "Pick out the Cup" that was hiding the walnut. It seemed easy. You just watched very carefully as the hustlers moved the nut from under one and another. For a buck you get to point to the cup hiding the nut. Of all people, I should know better than this. Like I said, I was not feeling too smart. I hate to admit it, but I was feeling lonely and depressed.

I wanted something to happen, even if it was not good for me.

There was a different con every ten or twenty feet. I was on the edge of fantasy, close to crossing over into believing it was all real. These guys were good. One guy yelling "Watch the Mouse!" It was real. Doing what the command was. Am I going off the edge? Is it real? I can't let this happen. My hands were shaking. I wanted to be back in the engine room.

"I should call Bob." No, I can't let anyone know I'm not as tough as I seem. Then I saw something that I needed, like a pet. A dancing Santa Claus. How can I make you believe this? I don't care. I bought it. Five Dollars, It's mine.

The guy was really good. He handed the box to me and said, "Shake it, don't break it."

I started walking back towards the Floral Studios. I was anxious to get back to my room. I kept thinking, "Am I crazy?" I'll just go with this for a while and then come back.

When I got back to the studio, it was late. The lobby was closed. There was a bell you could ring in case of an emergency. I went for the stairs. I wasn't going to get into that cage they called an elevator.

In the room I sat on the bed, staring at the box. I know this is not real, but I wanted to be disappointed. I'm not crazy.

Should I open the box? I thought of going back on the street, getting into a fight, maybe getting hurt. I never felt like this before. Do I need a doctor?

I went to the phone and called Bob. I never told him or anyone what I was going through until now. If I could analyze this I'm Okay. I felt I could turn this into a positive experience. I told Bob, "I'll see you on Fifty Seventh Street. We'll make the rounds."

We'll hit the agents. We'll pick up some work. Keep thinking positive thoughts. I'll get past this.

I decided to open the box. There, kind of crumpled up, was a red crepe paper Santa Claus. Well, I held it up by its head and let it go. It fell right to the ground. Then, I couldn't believe that I tried this, I picked it up, held it by its head and said out loud. "Shake it, but don't break it."

Of course, it fell to the ground. I started to laugh and for the rest of my life it was my little secret.

Whenever I'm going to be tempted by something new, a business, a sport, or like now, writing I say to myself under my breath, "Shake it but don't break it."

Herb Evans

Warren Street

Christmas is over. My Macy's job ended the week after New Year's. Bob and I went to lunch every day, spent more money than we earned. Had great discussions about movies: *On The Waterfront* with Marlon Brando, *East Of Eden* with James Dean were the favorites.

We talked about acting and what it took to get that level of performance. I was interested in acting, and this is the first time I thought it might be a possibility. Bob was in an acting class, a teacher he had in high school, Charley Shapiro. I joined the class also. We met at a studio one night a week, partnered up with another actor, and worked all week rehearsing a scene from a play to perform on Wednesday in class.

You had to develop a thick skin, the criticism was brutal. I met some good people who advised me how to get extra work in restaurants and bars.

80 Warren Street, a building on Lower Manhattan; you walk through the front door and you're in another world. You are in a rotunda going up six stories, balconies going around each floor with employ-

ment agencies all specializing in food and beverage service.

Down on the ground floor was a news and magazine stand. If you were called for a job and you happened to be downstairs, you heard your name loud and clear from one of the agencies that you signed up with. The jobs for lunch cost fifty cents to one dollar, fifty cents for a runner, meaning delivery to go. I liked doing the runner jobs, you just had to be fast. The more orders you got, the more tips you had at the end of a three-hour shift.

There are so many restaurants in New York, someone always needed an extra to fill in for a sick call. The other jobs took more experience, like sandwich, cold station, or a griddle man. You had to know the language. The first job I had was a soda jerk. A waitress called out, "Stretch four, seaboard."

I just stood there. The boss literally threw me out. The place was packed.

He screamed, "We have no time for this!"

"Stretch four, seaboard." meant four large cokes to go.

I was learning, and after about a week I could hold down a job for a couple hours. I was fired a few more times, but each time I knew the language better.

80 Warren Street was packed with actors and actresses looking for extra work. They would be carrying scripts under their arms. You couldn't get them

to reveal who was casting. Sometimes I would show up at an open call (that meant no agent). We called that a "cattle call". Most often it was a waste of time.

Bob was getting some TV work. Most of the shows were live, meaning the union was AFTRA, American Federation of Television. He was getting featured parts on Playhouse 90, Armstrong Circle Theatre, *Verdict Is Yours*, and soaps.

I was getting more experience in the restaurant business but kept going to acting class and doing an occasional play off-Broadway and way off-Broadway. I decided to learn how to tend bar. You couldn't fake that job.

Eighty Warren Street was great. For a couple of years, I worked a different place every day.

Now off to a new adventure. At this time, I had moved to Fifteenth Street Union Square, close to Greenwich Village. The Village was the perfect place for me theatrically, and it had lots of restaurants. I picked out a few places I thought would be fun to work in.

The Provincetown Landing was below street level on Bleeker and Thompson Streets. It was dark. There was this guy leaning on the bar reading a newspaper. I asked for the manager. He looked at me.

"Use your brains, kid, can't you see we're closed?"

"I'm looking for a bartending job."

He asked about experience – that stopped me in my tracks.

I said, "Look, you let me work with another bartender for a couple weeks, no pay, then you decide."

"I don't decide, that's not my job, but I'll talk to the boss. Come back around four."

I came back and met Louie Beneveger. He lived upstairs in the hotel. He said, "You work for no pay until you know what you're doing." Luckily, I could keep the tips. It took more than two weeks, but I didn't care. I realized that there's a lot more to it than making drinks.

Most of the places in this part of Greenwich Village were mob owned; you never knew who was the boss. I was really starting to feel comfortable. I felt like I was really lucky. The streets at night were busy, lots of kids, coffee shops packed, kids reading their poetry, strumming guitars. I was starting to get ideas for opening a place of my own. This was my showbiz.

I was getting good as a bartender. Everyone wants to know the guy that's going to make you feel good. You have to be pretty tuned in to what your client needs. Sometimes it's formality and other times its first name. Never talk politics or religion. Mostly, you listen.

The Provincetown Landing was the center of what they called "Little Italy". I was fascinated and was always observing. These guys were the same as the gangsters in the movies. I didn't know who came first, the street or the film. I tended bar there for a couple of years. At this time, I was twenty-four and looked younger; they always called me "Kid". One time I said, "My name is Herb."

I was told, "We like you, Kid, so that's good enough."

I liked being a bartender. It's like the bar itself was the boundary. I was on the outside of all that was going on, but I could see and hear.

One time Louie came in and said, "They need you at the 7 Steps, get over there fast."

The 7 Steps was a gay bar around the corner. Gay bars were illegal at that time, so they were all mob-owned. The place was packed and there was nobody behind the bar. I jumped in and got things smoothed out pretty quick. I loved being the hero, the trouble-shooter. I always showed up at the Landing and then they told me where I was needed.

In 1950 women weren't allowed to be behind a bar past midnight and last call was 4:00 a.m., so I found it lucrative to relieve a barmaid.

By midnight the money was flowing, most of the customers were feeling no pain. It was a stupid law and it wasn't fair. I made more money between midnight and 4:00 a.m. than their eight-hour shift.

This was perfect for me. I was still getting small parts in off-Broadway plays, most of the theaters were in the Village, so I could make it to the bar before midnight. Sometimes I would miss curtain call, but it didn't matter.

I was in some really good plays like *Camino Real* by Tennessee Williams. I played different parts – the thief, the mummer, the pilot on the Fugitivo. This play ran more than sixty performances. It beat the Broadway run.

My life was about to change. There was a club on Seventh Avenue South, upstairs at the Duplex. It had a small service bar, a small stage, and about forty seats, little cocktail tables. Downstairs was just a neighborhood bar. Jan Wollman ran the room upstairs and I became the bar guy. She booked the talent and served the drinks.

This was a great job for me, I loved going there. We didn't open till 11:00 p.m. I could still work some plays. I had a way of getting parts after they opened. I would talk to the stage managers, give my picture and made-up resume. These small parts were always becoming available, especially if it was a long run.

Monday, Broadway was dark, so that was a busy night for us. We made that guest night.

I was doing a play called *Driftwood*, way off-Broadway. An actress that worked with me came in on guest night. She wanted to sing. Bob Macnomy was the house piano player, he said he would accompany her.

She sat on top of the piano, cupped her hands, and sang *A Sleeping Bee in the Palm of My Hand.*

The room was shocked, her voice was pure but strong.

I didn't even know she could sing.

Herbert Jacoby was in the audience. He owned the Blue Angel, a club uptown. He wanted to sign her right then, but she was only eighteen and a senior in high school. Anyway, she got a Broadway show at her first audition.

This was the birth of Barbra Streisand.

Herb Evans

The Village Gate

The Provincetown Landing was on Bleeker and Thompson Street. Across the corner was the Old Mills Hotel. It was considered a flophouse.

For a couple of bucks, you could get a room and flop for the night. Art Delugoff took the basement and turned it into a nightclub called The Village Gate. It was a happening place, open till six in the morning. When we closed, that was the place to go. It featured folk music and calypso. I went down to hear this calypso singer, Harry Belafonte. Everyone knew this guy was special.

The Village was so exciting in the 50s and 60s. There was a coffee shop, The Gaslight Club. We got to see Bob Dylan at the start of his career. Personally, I didn't get what the fuss was, he couldn't sing that good. I was more into Sinatra. I guess I was what they called "square". It was later that I started to listen to his lyrics. I got that he was a brilliant poet who was saying important things that we all were feeling.

The stretch of Bleeker Street from East Broadway to Seventh Avenue South was vibrant with music, theater, poets, artists. Circle in the Square was the hot theater, playing Eugene O'Neil's *The Iceman Cometh* with Jason Robards, Jr.

To get to see actors with the power of George C. Scott, Jason Robards, Marlon Brando, Dustin Hoffman, Al Pacino and others performing on stage was electric.

I always felt blessed to be around at that time.

Gateway to the Arts

During the late fifties I was busy all the time. My friend, Bob was getting some feature roles on TV. He got me some small extra roles on live shows like *Armstrong Circle Theater* and *Playhouse Ninety*. These were quality shows that came under AFTRA, The American Federation of Television Artists. It was a good way to learn, but, it didn't pay much.

One of the shows was *The Engineer of Death* starring Telly Savalas. I was one of the Israeli Mosaad that captures Adolph Eichmann in Argentina and whisks him back to Israel for trial. I watched the featured actor. I was learning technical things, always be on your mark and play to the camera.

Another show was *Jail Break*. I had what was referred to as special business, a step up from standing in a crowd. When the escape started, prisoners were running across the yard. A ladder leaned against the wall.

I was to climb up and the guards push the ladder away from the wall. My special business was to hit the ground, roll over, get up, and run back.

As the saying goes, "the best laid plans..." I

sprained my ankle and didn't get up and run. The director raised the camera and saved the shot. To say I was embarrassed was an understatement.

I was also getting some extra film work. You didn't get to be a SAG member. For the Screen Actors' Guild you had to have lines.

I did one screen extra with Sofia Loren, in a film called *That Kind of Woman*. The extras were all soldiers lined up on a train platform with duffel bags. Along comes Sofia Loren, the most beautiful woman any of us had ever seen. It didn't take much acting on my part. It was real to me.

Another one was *The Rose Tattoo* with Anna Magnani. This was a screen play adapted from Tennessee Williams's *Orpheus Descending*. Starring with Magnani was Burt Lancaster. Seeing Lancaster up close was electrifying. I know what they mean when I hear star quality.

It was really magic. It's an X quality. You either have it or you don't. I never heard any one explain it.

It was at this time I met Cherry Davis at the Duplex. I was tending bar at this small club, trying to get noticed. She was playing Polly Peachum in Bertolt Brecht's *Threepenny Opera* at the Theater Dileze.

She was a triple threat, dancer, singer, and actor. We hit it off good, and were together for three years.

Now my introduction to the arts just went up to another level.

Cherry was a professional, a member of all the unions, and was signed with an agent and manager. We attended all the equity symposia on Broadway.

Now I was viewing all the geniuses of theater. Arthur Miller, Clifford Odets, Tennessee Williams, and Eugene O'neill.

Being part of the audience of equity members, listening to the greats sharing their process of creating, this was exciting times. There is a book sitting in the middle of all this.

The books are always written about the ones that make it. But, to tell the story of the inside, the crazy things that go on with the rest of us, that would be a more than a volume.

Eighty Warren Street, that's how we made our living. For me, that was the gateway to the arts.

Addicted to drama

I was twenty-two, living in a furnished room. Making sure I was availalble for work on Thanksgiving, Christmas Eve and Christmas Day.

I was always invited to friends' homes to participate in the festivities. I always made up a story why I couldn't come.

Working in restaurants on the holidays was the best. It was sad, and I loved every minute of it.

1955 to 1959 were the craziest four years of my life. I was doing off-off-Broadway plays, very small parts on television, working in restaurants, nightclubs, living an adventure. I woke up each day not knowing what to expect, adapting to anything that would come my way.

First thing in the morning, head to Fifty Seventh Street and Seventh Avenue, meet Bob, and make the rounds to casting agents, drop off pictures and resumes, living in the fantasy of walking into an office and being greeted with, "You're just what we're looking for!"

Well, that was naive and would never happen. After dropping off a few pictures and resumes, we'd jump down to the subway, get off at Houston Street, then walk a couple of blocks to 80 Warren Street, check in at a few agencies.

I was available for any kind of job: sandwich man, griddle cook, soda jerk, runner, waiter. It was now eleven a.m. and the restaurants would start panicking. Someone was always missing.

Eighty Warren Street was like going to Fordham, the premier restaurant management school.

Diary of a Bartender

Even though my time behind the bar was only about eight years out of more than eighty, it informed everything I have done. It's where I felt comfortable. Most people walk into a bar and in that moment are a little insecure. They have stepped onto a stage, and it's my stage. Everyone wants to know the bartender, or more importantly, they want the bartender to know them.

The minute you acknowledge your guests, they become part of the cast of this show. The best bartenders are not necessarily rated by their drink skill, although that's important.

The bartender that has extraordinary peripheral vision that can acknowledge a new patron, even though he or she is making a drink. Now that is a skill. Even though the bar is busy and it will take more than a moment to get to the new customer, it's forgiven when the customer feels comfortable that you know they're waiting.

Herb Evans

Greyhound

In 1956 I found myself broke in California. I had to get back to New York. I always felt if you can't make it in the Big Apple, you can't make it anywhere. Bob got me enough money to scrape a way to get back.

There was a guy taking passengers across the country. He had a 9-passenger station wagon. It was an old Plymouth. Gas was only 25 cents a gallon. This guy was a little nuts. He told me he was going to be like Greyhound. Within a year he would get another junk car.

He had eight passengers lined up, $50 apiece. This was definitely not first class. The passengers he had were European, very little English. A woman on one side of me had a ratty fake fur coat. I was squished in the middle. It took me a day to learn to breathe. Most of the passengers were getting off in Chicago. Me and an old guy were going to New York.

The driver was popping pills. His head was bobbing, and he was getting a little more crazy. He stopped for gas. That's when I told him I could drive for a while.

He went berserk, told me he was the captain and I was guilty of mutiny. Well, I couldn't get any sleep, I was keeping an eye on this guy. Driving pretty fast, the hood popped up and flew over our head. He stopped on the side and got the hood. We tied it down with some rope he had, then he said he couldn't make it to New York. Me and the old guy could take a train from Chicago.

Our captain would get us a ticket from our $50 fee. When we got to the main station in Chicago, he asked me to go in and find out the cost of the ticket to New York.

I said, "Are you nuts? The minute I step in that station, you will drive off. You go in and get the tickets." There was a cop standing on the corner, so he wasn't going to cause trouble. He went in and got the tickets.

I made it to New York and did all right. I don't think Greyhound has anything to worry about.

Homeless in Paradise

Bob decided to go to night court. He figured we could pick up mannerisms, speech, and different personality traits that could be helpful in our development as actors, sort of like packing our theater trunk.

Most night court participants were homeless, They were just trying to survive the harsh winter. Breaking and entering, petty thefts, it's pretty clear on the surface what this is all about, but these are human beings and their stories underlie each and every one of them.

This is the story of Roscoe and his girlfriend Evelyn. Roscoe was explaining to the judge that he had a lease to sleep in the men's room from twelve midnight to seven in the morning.

It's obvious that Roscoe had some mental problems, but it was also obvious that he was a gentle, sweet person. The bathrooms were located in the hallway. This was a low-cost housing project, a step up from being called flop housing.

The judge asked to see this lease, which of course was not legal. The manager of the building, his name was Lenny, showed up to speak for Roscoe. Lenny felt he had to do something, it was freezing out on the streets. But Roscoe and Evelyn were counting their blessings. Evelyn was seeing it like a two-room apartment with two bathrooms. Every morning they scrubbed and cleaned. The tenants on the floor were happy.

Bob and I were getting a lot more than experience to put into our theater box. This was a life lesson. Love, caring, commitment, could be found anywhere if you honor your life and choose to be blessed. Evelyn and Roscoe loved one another and we all felt better about ourselves.

A Taste of New York

Time to go to the automat. Five cents gets you a cup of hot water, then over to the condiments table, where a mixture of some ketchup and other spices got you a really good tomato soup. Then some saltine crackers. Yum. This was living.

Sometimes we would get vegetables, corn, carrots, peas, ten cents apiece served in a tiny bowl called a monkey dish. If I wasn't feeling up to par, I would get a couple of vegetables and put them in my soup. Now that vegetable soup would cure whatever ails you.

Most nights I was working a shift, taking a class or rehearsing a scene. Other times I would go to Nedick's, a great place to study people. Nedick's was a chain serving hot dogs. There was one on almost every corner. I would get a hot dog and stand at a counter facing outside.

At rush hour that's five to ten people moving along, covering the sidewalk. It was as graceful as a river. Then they would flow down the steps to the subway. That looked like a waterfall of people. You couldn't hear any sound coming from outside, so that added to the mystique. I found it fascinating. Sometimes you would get physical emotions, displaying frustration, anger, or surrender.

Everyone just facing forward, being carried along and then down. It was so tight that only from the waist up was visible. To keep warm, the heads were tucked below the collar of the coats. It was a bizarre sight. Down the stairs on the platform, everyone jockeying for position, the train pulls up, the screeching brakes hurt your ears. The doors slide open and you get carried on. People pressed against one another, sometimes like that for almost an hour, never talking, no eye contact. These are unwritten rules.

If you were lucky to get a seat, it was like being buried, people hanging from straps over you, the train jarring from side to side, getting ready for a stop. Everyone flying forward. Trying to maintain rhythm with your dance partner. The doors open, people fighting to get off. More getting off than on, finally, a breather. Smooth sailing from here.

Time to get over it

I found an apartment on First Avenue and Fourteenth Street. It was what they called a railroad. The rooms were lined up, so to get from the kitchen to the bathroom, you had to walk through the bedroom.

I was on the second floor. It was a pretty good deal, four rooms for $75 a month. The owner of the building had a furniture store on the ground floor. Outside the kitchen window was the roof of the ground floor store. I turned that into a deck. It was great to catch some sun. You just had to climb out the window.

This was when I was working at my first bartending job at The Provincetown Landing. I could walk to work, going through Washington Square Park where the most interesting things were going on day and night.

One time there was a crowd listening to Theodore Bickel, a great folk singer and a well-known actor. He put out some albums. One was titled *Songs of a Russian Gypsy*. He was fantastic. I could listen to him for hours. He was able to sing in twenty-seven different languages. He founded a repertoire theater in Israel and performed the classics in Hebrew. That's the kind of magic you could find in New York, great artists performing free, just for the love of it.

Another thing that was going on all the time was chess. There was a section with about a dozen tables and some very serious matches going on all the time. There would be a young kid playing an old person. It was fascinating. I learned the moves just by watching. Sometimes the greats like Bobby Fischer played there. He was world famous, then he went crazy.

One of the dance troupes I saw was called Inbal; they only came to this country once, and I was fortunate enough to see them. The group was from the desert on the southern part of Israel. They were Sephardic Jews, mostly black.

Walking down MacDougal Street, exotic-looking people with push carts loaded with fruits and vegetables. Poets reading their poetry. A horse-drawn wagon with a guy singing loudly, "I buy old clothes."

Now onto Bleeker Street, passing one of the best off-Broadway theaters, Circle in the Square. The show having a pretty good run was Eugene O'Neill's *The Iceman Cometh* with Jason Robards, Jr. Then passing Art Delugoff's Village Gate, I think I will stop there after I finish work.

The Provincetown Landing was below street level. The whole area was overrun with rats. I would open and turn on the lights, you could hear them scampering for cover. I had to go another level down to tap the kegs of beer, that was scary. The kegs were on a dirt floor, we had planks of wood to walk on, it was damp and dimly lit. Some of the rats seemed to be as big as cats.

2:00 a.m., closed up, still going to see what's happening at the Gate. Just in time to catch the last set of Leon Bib.

Life is good.

Herb Evans

Diary of a Bartender

A New York Story

I was walking up Sixth Avenue towards Central Park feeling a little down – less than depressed, but definitely not happy. This mood is rare for me, as I am an optimist, mostly thinking that something is around the next corner that could be life-changing – either a bullet or being discovered for something.

I felt like I was floating along not really touching the ground. That feeling was a recurring dream.

My girlfriend Cherry Davis was on the road starring in *Hail the Conquering Hero*, co-starring Eddie Bracken. This was out-of-town tryouts – Boston, Philly, Washington, then Broadway. The show was not being well received. They kept making changes, trying to fix it. That's Broadway – it's brutal.

They finally brought in a show doctor. These are specialists that can fix a show. When they got to Boston, a discussion was made, a new concept, a new actress. It didn't work. The show closed after a couple of weeks on Broadway. Cherry was devastated, but as they say, "that's show biz."

Back to Sixth Avenue, a bunch of teenagers just got out of school, going crazy, changing the mood.

143

One of the kids stole an apple from a fruit pushcart. I was immediately judging the whole scene. It was more fun to steal the apple than eat it. Crossing the wide Central Park South, the kids were heading to Sheep Meadow, a peaceful break from the steaming city.

That's what I needed. I started to think, Cherry Davis has been either on Broadway or off, working for years. She was eight years older than me. To her mind, she hadn't made it. It became clear to me, I'd better get a business open, I can't count on show biz.

I sat down on a bench at Sheep Meadow, nice, but the pack of teens was carrying on. They were playing catch with the stolen apple. Opposite me lying on a bench was a man that looked like he had been on the street for quite a while. He had packages tied up in bundles. I figured he had all he owned with him.

The kids were still throwing the apple. One threw wild and it landed in the grass next to the homeless guy. I assume he was homeless. There were so many homeless that people would just step over them lying in doorways.

The man picked up the apple and handed it to the kid, the same kid that stole it. It seems like a long time ago. Something happened in that moment – they stood there facing one another. I stood across from them, frozen. Whatever happened, it was quick and I felt like I was part of it.

The kid handed the apple to this guy and went back to his tribe. The man stood there looking at the apple with a slight smile. He wiped it clean and put it in his pack. He gathered his stuff and walked off.

I never forgot that kid, he showed compassion, even love. This was a gift to me, a small moment of compassion, that changed my mood. An apple around the corner.

Herb Evans

Night in the Village

2:00 a.m. the bars are giving last call. The streets are packed, there's a line outside Pam Pam All-Night Breakfast Place. I just closed the Provincetown Landing. It was a crazy night – a couple of fights, I'm thankful it's over.

Wrapping up the money in a bank bag to take it upstairs to my boss, Lui Benvenger. I knock, he cracks open the door, lying in bed. I hand him the bag, he puts it under his pillow and slams the door. The only thing he ever says to me is, "Everything okay? See you tomorrow."

When you work an eight-hour shift at high speed, it takes a while to unwind. The street is high energy. I sensed there's volatility in the crowd. You feel it – time to get out of the way. It's a skill, we called it street smarts.

I'm finally getting in for some food. I run into some friends, there's an extra chair, it's good to sit down. The conversation is show biz mixed with bar biz. The uniform cop on the beat walks in, a nice guy.

He comes over, "How you guys doing?" It's good

to see him, he takes the edge off. I'm relaxing a little. Beat cops look out for us, it's a neighborhood thing. I miss that in today's world. On the way out, he turns. "It's wild out there, be careful going home." I usually walk home. I live on Fourteenth Street and First Avenue and I'm on Seventh Avenue South and Eighth, about ten blocks.

Tonight, I think I'll grab a subway and get off at Fourteenth and walk a few blocks. I get home exhausted. I'm out as soon as I hit the pillow.

I'm up early to meet Bob. We're going to make the rounds to agents with pictures and resumes. I meet him on Fifty Seventh Street at the corner drug store. The first thing he says is, "Did you hear about last night?"

"No, what?"

"Some drunk threw a chair through the front window of Pam Pam's, caused a riot, and seriously injured three people. Ambulances, police, it was nuts."

I must have just missed it.

I'm getting to the point, that every time I go out I think of the possibility of disaster. Do I really want to live this way? I never gave a lot of thought to how fragile life is, even during my Navy service. I was thinking about it now. I didn't talk about it to anyone.

Things changed.

I changed, I couldn't sit on the train unless I was

facing the entire car. When I was in crowds, which was often, I was constantly looking around. It became obvious. I finally told Bob. He talked me into seeing a counselor. It was bringing up things that I didn't even know I was holding onto. I finally got to a point of acceptance. Yes, it's fragile, and that's life. So what? Be careful. Today we're told, "See something, say something" – the way it's always been.

Survival

I just remembered getting a job outside of the food industry. I read that the post office was hiring temporary Christmas help. It would be ten days, and the money was good. My idea was to work ten days and have enough money for at least a month. I was pretty excited about it, so that night I ran it by Bob. He thought it was crazy, and it took a lot of arguing back and forth. He finally said, "Okay, let's go for it."

We both got hired and reported to the main post office on Thirty Fourth Street. That was before automation, so we were seated on stools in front of what they called "pigeonholes."

Our job was to put envelopes with corresponding numbers into the pigeon slots. Nothing could be more boring than that.

Bob was really bitching: "Look what you got me into."

I said, "Let's make it fun."

I put my feet up and was sailing the envelopes into the slots. The supervisor came up behind me and kicked the stool right out from under me. I went flying on my butt. Well, that required a response

that got me escorted out. I waited about ten minutes, and out came Bob.

He was laughing. "You talked me into that job,
I wasn't going to stay while you escaped!" I started
to laugh also as we headed down the subway to 80
Warren Street. It was still early enough to pick up a
lunch job.

Tour Guide

I answered an ad to be a tour guide. The woman behind the desk asked my date of birth, 8-10-33. She started to write different numbers down and then she told me she was a numerologist. I'd never heard of that before, so many strange people in the city. She told me that I wasn't right for this type of work.

I really needed the job, it was perfect, only about three hours a day. She was trying to book a tour for that afternoon. She said, "I'm sure this is a mistake, but I'll take a chance." I got all the information and a hat that said New York Tour Guide. I was to go down to the subway to the Astor Hotel and meet the group. It was sixty students and two teachers.

We were to take the IRT Train to the Battery, Lower Manhattan, then get a ferry to the Statue of Liberty. I was surprised that I had never been to the Statue before. It's a small island in the Hudson River, halfway to New Jersey.

When I got to the hotel they were all lined up in the lobby. The group was from the Midwest. This was a really big deal for them.

I wanted to make this a memorable and fun experience. I told them to follow me down the stairs to the train station. One teacher was in front and one in back. The kids were lined up in twos. The noise and the crowds of people gave them a taste of New York.

The train pulled up to the platform and the New Yorkers pushed their way to the front, as New Yorkers do. The doors opened and I said, "Follow me." As soon as I got into the train with just a few of the kids, the doors closed.

About twenty kids and one teacher were still on the platform. I yelled through a window, "Don't move, I will get the next train back."

We got to the next stop. I didn't make the same mistake, I held the doors open until I got my students and teacher on the platform. Now we had to go upstairs and take the walkway to the other side, get the train back, and then do the same thing.

When we got back, the students that were told to not move were standing almost at attention. There was fear on their faces. I told them, "We're all good and that won't happen again."

This time I got them all in before I let the doors close. We got to our stop and went upstairs out into the fresh air. There was the Statue of Liberty. And there was the ferry on its way to the island. We had missed our ride. Well, I apologized and told them we had to get back to the hotel. They had another tour to go on. I told them the view of the statue was as good as being there.

Their next adventure was the Empire State Building, at that time the tallest in the world. The guide to take them was waiting in the lobby, a really tall guy. I thought to myself, he's right for this job, I wonder when he was born. Back at the office, I turned in my hat. The woman just looked at me.

I said, "I know, my numbers were wrong."

Summer

I was still in Charlie Shapiro's acting class, going down to 80 Warren Street, picking up extra jobs in the restaurant business. I had heard from my theater friends that they would go up to the Catskill Mountains in Upstate New York, work the whole summer, and come home with enough money to make it through the winter, and only have to pick up an extra job once or twice a week.

I went up to Parksville, New York. There was an employment agency that staffed the hotels. I showed up a couple of weeks before the season started. I didn't have any experience, so I thought of the cliché "Early bird gets the worm."

The agency sent me to the Concord, a big fancy place. I was hired as an assistant waiter, that meant I carried the trays and the main waiter served the food. The dining room was huge, but very few patrons were there yet. I was given a bunk in a barracks-type setup. You get up at 6 a.m. and show up in the dining room. You take orders from your manager (that's the waiter you work for). Breakfast was served from 8 a.m. to 10 a.m. Then you set up for lunch. It's a 12 to 14-hour day. There's no time to spend money. Room and food are free. You get your tips when your guests check out.

I felt a little more comfortable after about ten days. The season was about to start, more guests were arriving, then I was called into the office and was told the steady employees had arrived and I wasn't needed. I was furious. I was used, and they knew all along I wouldn't work the season.

At that time of my life, I was a little hot-headed. I went back to the dining room and messed up the tables that I set up for lunch. I was angry that they used me, but it was foolish to act out like I did. I went back to the agency to get placed again.

This was a small town and the word was already out, watch out for that kid. It took a little diplomacy and I spent some groveling time, but the agent said, "I'll give you one more chance."

He said there's a spot open at the Lash Hotel, a much smaller family place. The job is tough, nobody wants it. You'll be working the children's dining room. Forty kids in high chairs, we called them the high chair cases. I was up for this. If I could get these kids to eat and be happy, I would control the room. The mothers would come in and tell me what their kid needed, it was bizarre.

The moms were nervous and unsteady and created lots of screaming. Sometimes I would walk out of the kitchen with a tray stacked with 10 dishes and moms would literally attack, and the tray would be empty before I could set it down.

The hotel had a counselor for the kids between meals, a young guy, Barry Primus, who had a magic way with kids. He played the guitar and sang, and the kids were mesmerized. I got friendly with him and had a great idea. This could be really lucrative, and we could control the situation.

The parents loved the idea of Barry working with me at mealtime, anything to make their summer more pleasurable. I had a meeting with all the parents and they agreed to increase the gratuity. Barry and I split the tip at the end of each week. No one wanted to mess with our arrangement.

The management was happy that they didn't have to deal with the high chair room. We had so much control that there were a few moms taking suggestions from us, like don't come in until we get the food to the kids. It became a win-win – we made more money than the main dining room waiters, and we controlled the room. The kids were happy, they loved Barry, and he always had some surprise for them. I learned a lot from this experience.

Barry became a pretty well-known character actor, I've seen him in some movies, like *New York, New York* with Robert De Niro and *Absence of Malice* with Paul Newman, to name a few. He is also on TV quite a bit.

A very memorable summer indeed.

A Night to Remember

I went down to 80 Warren Street to pick up an extra job. It was so great to have a building with employment agencies all specializing in the food and beverage business. I could work whenever I wanted.

I was registered with a number of different agencies. The building was a huge rotunda with balconies circling up six levels. On the ground there was a newspaper stand. You could get a cup of coffee and a magazine. Billy the Man, that's what we called him, "Billy the Man" – it was his concession.

He was supposedly blind, but I doubt it. Don't try to take anything off the stand without dropping some coin. Billy the Man would get you.

I went up and checked in. I was known by this time, so I'd just hang out downstairs and wait for my name to be called. I never knew where I would be going. They would call me for any job from short order cook to soda jerk. I got called for a bartender, that was lucky for me. It was a busy place, good money. It was for evening. I didn't have to be there till 6:00, so I could pick up a lunch job. Looks like this is going to be a really good day.

Time to go to the bar job. It was in Brooklyn. I got the BMT to Gravesend Neck Road, then a bus transfer to Gerritsen Beach, then walked a couple of blocks to San Chels Restaurant. I was never in the place before, but it looked pretty expensive. They gave me a black Eisenhower jacket and a cummerbund. I had a white shirt and a black bow tie.

The place was not my taste, the walls were covered with smoked mirrors and the lighting was crystal chandeliers. They told me to meet the bartender and he would tell me what the deal was. He said, "Just do what I say."

The station I had was some stools and a service area. I had to get the drinks for the waiters. The place was starting to fill up and it was becoming obvious this was a wise guy scene.

I recognized some of the crowd from Greenwich Village. We had a huge tip cup on the back bar. I had a feeling I wouldn't have to work for a few days after this night.

On my end was a banquette with a round table that could seat ten. It looked like a serious meeting was taking place.

There were six guys, then four guys came in and went straight to the table. They all stood up and greeted the new comers with total respect.

The bartender came over to me and said, "I'll take care of this, you work the other side." It was now about 10:00 pm and the place was packed.

There was one really loud guy buying drinks for people and running up quite a tab. The guy who I assumed was the boss called me over to the corner of the bar and told me to lay the tab right in front of the loud guy.

Well, this guy picks up the bill and tears it to pieces and throws it in my face. Then he hands me a $100 bill. He says, "Put that in the cup, not the register."

I looked at the boss and made a gesture like, "What do you want me to do?" He said, "What do you want me to do?" and walked away.

A few minutes later we heard a shot. My partner pulled me down to the ground and said "Don't move until I tell you."

It seemed like time stood still until he said, "Okay." I stood up and the place had emptied out. There was a body in front of the bar. My partner said, "Just go home, and, take the cup." It was 2:00 a.m.

When I got home I was exhausted. There was no paperwork on me so I figured we'd chalk it up as a bad dream.

The next morning there's a knock at my door. It's two detectives. They said we have to go down to the station.

I told them, "Look I'm just an actor working extra jobs."

When we got downtown it looked like everyone

that was at the bar was there.

The guy that was killed was Johnny Roberts, alias Johnny Roberlito, alias John the Mortician. He owned a mortician parlor in the Village. The guy that shot him was Joey Gallo, who was killed not too long after.

He was the guy that gave me the $100 tip.

A night to remember!

The Year I Met Pat

The Duplex was becoming known as the stepping stone for talent to try out new material. Woody Allen came in. He was a comedy writer for Sid Caesar and others. He was not doing standup. He was a wreck. We had to push him out on stage, but his nervousness carried into his act and it worked.

I was getting obsessed more and more with opening my own place. It was on my mind all the time. I decided it was time for me to start working in uptown places where I could get closer to possible investors. It sounds like I was becoming a pain in the ass, but it wasn't like that, I wasn't aggressive. If someone was interested in me, then conversation would start.

I got a lunch job in a fast lunch place, Mahue's Country Kitchen on Madison Avenue and Sixty Ninth Street – the most exclusive shops and buildings. People would ask me, "What are you really? A student?" I would always answer, "At this moment I am a server, but I have some ideas."

I was still at The Duplex. Jan told me she had some new people coming in, George Segal and Pat

Scott had an act that was hilarious. He played banjo and they both sang. Pat was the ex-wife of George C. Scott. I was hoping he would come in. He was the new toast of Broadway, great actor.

Cherry Davis had the ingénue lead in *Three Penny Opera* by Kurt Wyle. She was a triple threat dancer, singer, and actress. The minute I saw her my heart pounded a little faster. She had a big gummy smile and long red hair. Jan looked at me and laughed.

"Herb, let's make drinks and get through the night." When the place was closing, Cherry and I went to an all-night joint for some late supper. We were together for three years.

I was too young and immature to handle that kind of relationship. She was on the road in *West Side Story* when I realized this can't work.

I knew what it takes to be a success on stage, the sacrifice and commitment to study, and then the odds were against you. I loved the theatre and had too much respect for it to treat it like I wasn't all in.

In 1961, I met Pat. She was studying fashion at an exclusive school a few blocks down from where I was working. We hit it off pretty good. I was ready to go on a road trip to California. She said, "Take me with you, I have a VW Bug," so off we went.

I had no real reason for going except Bob had gotten married to a California girl and moved out there. He was getting a few movies and TV roles. Pat had to return to New York. There was school, and she was still living with her parents.

I stayed for a in L.A. for a while, but it was a disaster. L.A. was spread out; you couldn't get by the way I did in New York. There was more happening in one New York neighborhood than all of L.A. New York was definitely home.

Pat and I got to be close. It was getting serious; her mother wasn't too happy about it. Her father got interested in anything I liked, books, plays, music he wanted to talk about. I became the son he wanted.

Pat and I got married. There were problems that were way over my head. After a year, we got pregnant. Shelley was born in 1963. I was working at the Sign of the Dove. I was the head bartender, things felt good to me, but I was not aware of problems with Pat.

She was drinking privately. I later found out that alcohol addiction is a disease. You'd think that being in the bar business, I would be understanding about all this. To me, you either were a drunk or you weren't. Pat had the disease, she was an alcoholic. She was what they called a functioning alcoholic, so we didn't deal with it. In 1966 Samantha was born; I had two beautiful girls.

At that time Lincoln Center for the Performing Arts was under construction. Philharmonic Hall was complete, the restaurant and bar were operating and run by Stouffer's, a chain operation.

They were losing money. Their concept didn't work. A new food company, Luis Sherry, took over. Sherry's was a famous catering company. They were looking for a manager. I didn't think I had a chance, but I went up for an interview anyway.

The restaurant was a large open space in Philharmonic Hall, about 300 seats and a large bar. I went in about four nights before my interview, watching the operation and taking notes. I went in to meet Carl Rochell, the president of the company. His office was in the Plaza Hotel. This was a big-time business. I felt I had a lot to learn.

I sat down and faced Mr. Rochell. He looked over my resume and fired some questions at me: "How much yield in a #10 can of peas? What happens to a prime rib out of the oven? Does a steak continue to cook when it's sitting on the plate?"

Well, I was ready to walk out, but I said, "Look, Mr. Rochell, I know you're scraping the bottom of the barrel with me. But I made some notes.

"We are located in a theater, and the other buildings are under construction. The problem that Stouffer's had and you are having is that you are running by the traditional book. Well, the book hasn't been written for this operation.

"We have 2800 seats in the hall and an intermission, all coming out for a drink and a smoke. Lincoln Center is a nonprofit, and we are for profit. There is revenue that is coming at us, and we are looking the other way."

He said, "There are lots of restrictions here, you have to be careful." Then he surprised me. He said, "I'm going to give you a shot at it."

The next three years were filled with excitement.

Top of the Mountain

Working as a bartender in a Swiss restaurant in Greenwich Village on Eighth Street, we had to wear lederhosen and a hat with a feather. The owner was hooked on horse racing and was heavily in debt to the local bookie. Business was pretty good if the boss could break his gambling addiction.

My friend Bob was working the floor, I was on the bar. One day we came to work and there was a jukebox being brought in. We knew things were going downhill. The way the mob took over was to let you borrow money and you got deeper and deeper. Then they took over. The known collector in the neighborhood, Pipey, was always hanging at the bar. Bob and I were deciding whether to keep working there.

Business was getting slim.

We had an idea to turn it into a dinner theater. Pipey took us to his boss to make our pitch. His boss was a known capitán from Sullivan Street, he was a no-nonsense guy and he just said, "Go for it." We changed the concept from Swiss menu to American.

It was so good to get out of the lederhosen and

that ridiculous hat. Now we had to work on a play. We selected a one-act by Tennessee Williams, *Twenty Seven Wagons Full of Cotton*. This was made into a movie called *Baby Doll* with Eli Wallach. Bob wanted to direct, I was doing the lead, a guy with attitude, Sylva Vicarro. A really good actress, Tina Mandress that we knew from class, would play Baby Doll. We made flyers to pass around the Village. We got some kids to help us put up a couple of theatrical lights. No one was paid, but this was really exciting.

The show would start at nine. We would work the restaurant until 8:00 pm, then get ready to perform. Pipey was taking an interest in our progress. He kept asking how we were coming along. I'm sure he was told to keep an eye on us. Pipey got his name because he always carried a small lead pipe in his back pocket. If you were in debt and scheduled to pay, Pipey would show up. He rarely had any problem. Anyway, we had fun. No money, but fun.

Bob was a good director and he liked doing it. We decided to always keep a couple of one-act plays ready to go. The Top of the Mountain was going nowhere, there was tension in the Village, and it was time to get out of harm's way. We worked on another one-act called *I'll Take You*, a two-character original written by a friend.

We performed it in schools and a convalescent home. Being in our 20's with boundless energy, definitely happy times. We always had a place to be, things to do, making the rounds to casting agents, going down to 80 Warren Street to pick up a lunch job. Some of the jobs that the agent at 80 Warren Street sent us to were crazy.

At Christmas there were jobs everywhere.

One time I was sent up to a restaurant called The Studio. They had a central kitchen and three different rooms, fine dining, a nightclub with dance floor, and a jazz room. I was assigned to the dining room. It was tray service. I picked up the food in the kitchen and went down the hall and came out in the jazz room. It was like I was in a strange place with a tray full of main dishes.

In those days there was no such thing as an H.R. person. Some of the chefs were like stars, and you could suffer some serious abuse from them. I was pretty good at scoping out the kitchen, knowing what I had to deal with.

Another restaurant that was on my resume was The Terrace, at the U.N. on Forty Second Street and the East River, the owner was a retired Army captain. He ran this place like a drill sergeant. The place was packed every day at lunch, mostly diplomats from the U.N.

Mr. Depalmer, the owner, would line us up before we opened and inspect us. We had to be spotless. He'd look at our nails and our shoes had to be shined. He was definitely still the captain in the Army.

All these different jobs were great training for the next phase of my life. It seems that I have been in training all my life.

A Moment on Broadway

I went to see *The Miracle Worker* with Anne Bancroft as Anne Sullivan and Patty Duke as Helen Keller. That was the most powerful, moving theater I had ever experienced.

The first act, Patty Duke was a wild, untrained animal. The audience was gasping at the physical performance, the frustration of this young girl being portrayed. She was literally throwing her body across the stage. There was excitement, Helen's teacher Anne Sullivan was arriving. Anne Bancroft played her with great strength but also love and commitment. I felt frozen in my seat. It was amazing, as intense as a mystery. How can this work? How can Helen connect the signing to an object? Not hearing, not seeing, is it possible?

After the painstaking process of establishing a relationship, during the frustration of not getting success Helen runs off the front porch and falls next to the water pump. Anne follows her and grabs her hand and puts her hand in hers. She signs "water" with one hand and pumps water with the other. At that moment, you can see on Helen's face, she gets it, and with distortion yells "wa wa", and the world opens up for her.

    The curtain comes down and it's intermission.
    The audience is just sitting, not moving.
    Suddenly they erupt into a standing ovation.
    No one took the intermission.
    I never saw anything like that before or after.
    The true power of theater.

California

There was a business in New York called Caravan Cars. If you qualify, you get a car to deliver across the country. Bob and I got a Cadillac Eldorado to drive to Los Angeles and get it to the owner there.

We planned it out, I would drive for eight hours, then he would do the same. That way we could get there in a couple of days. The first night I was driving, Bob was asleep in the back. On Route 66, for a stretch it was two lanes. I pulled off to the left to get gas, pulled back on the highway, smooth sailing.

I saw some headlights coming toward us. I suddenly realized that when I left the gas station, the highway became four lanes and I was on the wrong side going about 70 miles an hour.

I turned the car to the right, hit the center divider, and went airborne, just like a movie. Bob hit the roof and I pulled off and stopped. The windshield was cracked and I am sure there was other damage under the car. We could have had a serious head-on. The car seemed okay enough to drive. We didn't have money to repair the windshield.

We got to Las Vegas. I had never seen anything

like this before. Bob wanted to check out a casino.

Pulling into the parking lot, I never saw so many lights. It was about 2 a.m. and it felt like daytime. Getting out of the car, Bob spotted a $20-dollar bill lying on the floor. He was convinced that this was a sign – we were going to get rich. Walking into the casino was another world, slot machines, dice tables, roulette, bright lights. I was not comfortable and fast getting a headache. Bob wanted to roll the dice, the table was crowded, but he squeezed in.

I stood back and watched. It took about 5 minutes and the $20 was gone. So much for the sign! The gambling fever got him crazy. I never witnessed anything like it. He wanted to put the car up for collateral and gamble. He tried to convince me that we would win. I tried to convince him that we would end up in jail.

I won that argument, but it took him a little time to get over it.

Diary of a Bartender

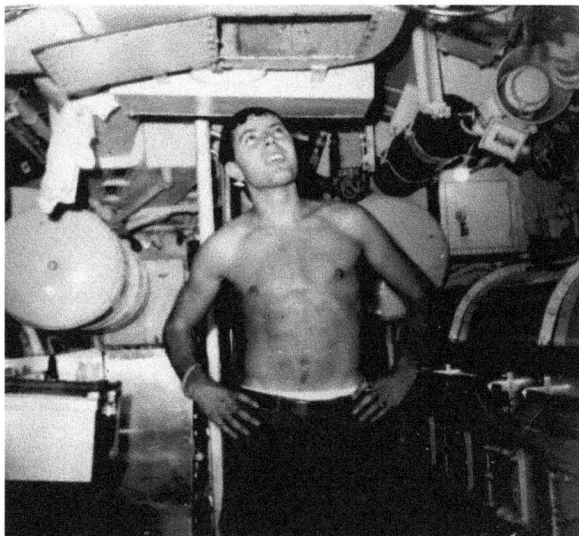

Herb Evans on the USS Sea Cat SS399 - 1939

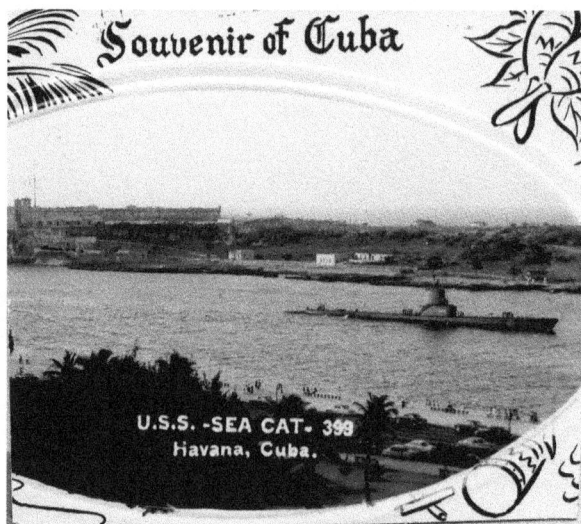

Souvenir of Cuba

U.S.S. -SEA CAT- 399
Havana, Cuba.

USS Sea Cat entering Havana Harbor, Cuba

Below: Appearing as the office vamp in a summer stock production of The Desk Set *in 1957, when she was fifteen, Barbara dances with Paul Bressoud. A critic called her "a fine young comedienne."*

Right: Barbara rehearses with Herb Evans for the way off-Broadway production of Driftwood, *December 1958.*

Charles Biasiny-Rivera

Courtesy Emily Cohb

January 1959: Barbara graduated from Erasmus Hall High School half a year early, and with a 91 average. She shocked her classmates by dating a black boy.

Courtesy Kevin Burns

Driftwood, Herb Evans performing with Barbra Streisand, 1959

Herb Evans

1960's

Danny Lavetso's P.J. Clark

Only in New York – the best place for burgers, drinks, and atmosphere, Danny Lavetso's P.J. Clark on Third Avenue and Fifty Ninth St., the Gold Belt.

Some developers wanted to buy P.J. Clark's to demolish it and put up a skyscraper. Danny would not let that happen, so the developers came up with buying the airspace over P.J.'s. They gave Danny $3,000,000 after taxes. They put up a building without touching P.J.'s, a landmark, still the best burgers and drinks. Who would have thought you could sell the airspace over an old burger joint?

"Only in New York."

Working Hard and Moving Up

I worked at The Sign of the Dove, a prestigious restaurant and bar on Third Avenue, the elevated train used to go down Third Avenue. It was a low-rent district. When the El was torn down, Third Avenue became the Gold Belt.

Dr. Santo bought a tenement building and gutted it, and over a year created The Sign of the Dove. I was lucky to be able to observe and learn. When he opened, I became the bar manager. This position was the top of the game for me. It was always, "Where do I go from here?"

This was the last stop in the bar position.

Although I took a pay cut, I knew I was going to be exposed to an exciting environment and a great opportunity. After the first year, I was made Vice President in charge of Food and Beverage. Special events had to be approved by Jos Salyer for safety concerns.

There was an interesting dynamic between us. He worked for Lincoln Center, a non-profit. I worked for Luis Sherry's, hopefully a for profit organization. What tied us together, that thread, was the patron of the arts. Whatever event was put on, it was to raise money for the Philharmonic, the ballet, the Music Center, also political functions.

In retrospect, I was moving too fast. I lacked humility, was starting to believe my own press. Planning my first restaurant, lining up possible investors, using my position with Sherry's. You can question the ethics about this, spending time promoting myself while on the payroll of Luis Sherry's.

Lincoln Center Years

Eric Leinsdorf, Conductor of the Boston Symphony, tried out something new. Classical orchestra music was not reaching a large portion of the possible audience, so the Boston Symphony designed the Boston Pops, an informal party atmosphere, reasonably priced.

It was successful, and Lincoln Center thought it should be tried there. There was a lot of effort to expand and dispel the snooty reputation that symphonies had. Leonard Bernstein started youth concerts on Saturday matinées. It was great to see these kids being exposed to this music and atmosphere. It was decided to get the Boston Symphony to come down to New York.

Eric Leinsdorf would conduct, I was invited to attend all the logistics meetings. We pulled out all the seats in the orchestra and built platforms to hold small cocktail tables. Each table had four chairs. We designed rolling carts to hold ice and bottles of champagne. There would be a cart for every row of tables. Sold out, we would serve 700 people. We would have two waiters assigned to each cart.

It was tricky, the service had to be done in a twenty-minute intermission. One more service at the conclusion. It was very festive and the patrons seemed to be having a great time.

Only one mishap, which we thought was pretty funny, at least some of us did. Bill Shuman, the President of Lincoln Center and a famous composer in his own right, gave us a pep talk. We all gathered before we opened. Mr. Shuman made a point of the danger of champagne corks flying. Unbelievable as this is, one cork went flying and landed on Bill Shuman's head, and there wasn't any hair to soften the blow.

It was really exciting that different things were tried. We had Japan Week with Ozawa conducting. I set up a Japanese buffet and went to the Japanese Consulate and got cooperation. We had a Japanese chef; all the servers wore "happy coats".

John D. Rockefeller, the Chairman of the Board, we used to call him the Old Man, was coming around more often. One time he showed up for dinner and all the tables were full. I apologized and said we didn't expect him. He was so happy to see the crowds, he said, "Herb, see if anyone would share a table." I mean, really, this was John D. Rockefeller.

Manhattan Blackout

1963, the year my first daughter Rochell arrived, now called Shelley. The first few years I called her Rocky until she told me enough of that. It also is the year I started work at Lincoln Center – a very busy year.

Shelley was born November 11. Sixteen days later John F. Kennedy, was assassinated. In 1966, my second daughter Samantha, known to most as Sam, was born.

Bobby Kennedy, Martin Luther King Junior, Kent State. The late 60s and 70s seemed crazy. I never thought it would settle down. Is it ever going to be peaceful again?

During this time, Lincoln Center was new and exciting and still being constructed.

In 1965, Manhattan was thrown into a blackout. The streets were immediately crowded with old air raid wardens with flashlights left over from the Second World War. The theaters were emptied out quickly.

Strangely, there was a lot of laughter going on. Maybe not so strangely. After all, this was New York.

A study conducted by NYU said that a year later there was a record number of babies born. Like I said, this is New York.

After everything settled down, people were served coffee or tea. We had cases of votive candles, so enough light. I grabbed a case of candles and walked the three blocks to the Dorchester Towers and then up twenty-six floors. Oh, how good it is to be young! Over the years we have had a number of blackouts, it happened more some time back. When you think about it, it's an engineering feat to power a city that goes up as much as it goes underground.

At Lincoln Center

During this time, I kept increasing the gross by finding new revenue streams. I put buffet tables on the three tiers of the hall, we lined up 500 champagne glasses filled halfway. When I gave the word, the waiters poured. The doors opened and every glass went for $1.00 each. Jos Salyer, the manager of Philharmonic, was furious. He said I couldn't just do what I wanted. There wasn't one glass broken, and these patrons of the arts loved it. Jos was getting letters of praise for the new service.

We were getting inquiries about doing special events. The Metropolitan Opera was under construction, over 3,000 seats. Then the New York State Theatre, another 2,800 seats. I was becoming the only person to talk to for events that required food and beverage. Pretty heady stuff for a young guy. I was meeting with high society. Mr. Rochell started lending me his secretary to attend meetings. She would type up agreements that I dictated. Dorothy made me sound so legal.

The events were always figured out to be a markup of 50 percent. That meant rental of equipment, labor, food, whatever it took to make an event memorable. The New York State Theatre was to hold the ballet company directed by George Balanchine.

I wish I could have worked with the architect. Function and flow of traffic seemed to be sacrificed for cosmetic beauty.

There was a large promenade on the second level. I was designing a function to benefit the ballet. The board wanted a sit-down at round tables. There was no way of getting from the back of the house to the promenade.

I rented forklifts with operators and had them lift the tables up to the portico outside the building all set up with silver, flowers, complete set-ups, waiters were lined up to take the tables off the lifts, two waiters for each round, carrying them into the promenade to marked tape on the floor. It was precision. If this didn't work, I was finished.

We had rolling carts heated with Sterno, with the food already on the plates. Everything had to be complete before the show ended.

We were like an army, everyone had a specific function. We rehearsed this for a couple of days ahead. Fred Staton, my assistant and Maître d', conducted the waiters and bussers like a field commander.

The chef was at the heating carts supervising the servers picking up the food. The doors opened, the show was over, 800 people came pouring out. Only half of them had an invitation card to get past the velvet ropes to the seating area. These were the large donors, the patrons of the arts.

The fund-raiser got as much press as the ballet. It was a success. To clean up and get everything back to get picked up by the rental company took as much work as the set-up. I had a separate crew to handle that.

Every charity, heart fund, cancer fund, music theater, political event, wanted to be at Lincoln Center. I was getting pretty well known, and I must admit, it went to my head a little bit. There were times when I had functions going in three buildings at the same time.

We were setting up in the Philharmonic for a big opening of *Night of the Iguana*, the film with Liz Taylor and Richard Burton. They were in the green room where the stars stayed in comfort before the show. We had not had a film before, this was new. Richard Burton kept calling for another bottle of vodka. After three bottles I called Jos Salyer and we went back to see if there was a party going on. It was just the two of them, totally drunk.

Jos and I, after a rough start, became good friends. We'd go across the street for a drink at the end of a crazy night to unwind. The Ginger Man was on Sixth Street, a popular pub. On the corner of Sixty Fourth and Broadway was an old supermarket. It was really out of place, surrounded by trendy theaters and shops. I didn't mention it to Jos, but every time we walked by, my creative juices would flow. This was it – I had to find out what the deal was.

I had a great job. Because I was running so many functions, Sherry's gave me a promotion, Vice President of all food and beverage. No more money, but an ego boost. Mr. Rochell got me business cards and some perks. Becoming Vice President was exactly what I needed to get investors for my first place. This was a wild idea. I mean, it wasn't starting off small, this was 185 feet of front footage on Broadway.

Pat's dad advised me how to form a Sub-Chapter S corporation. He also recommended an attorney. Having him to lean on was a great gift. I was going into the market every day, visually seeing the flow. I found out there was no lease, it was month-to-month. The process of negotiating with the owner of the building was slow and tedious. I gave Sherry's a year's notice, they were not happy. I swore to myself that if I ever had an employee that gave notice and wanted to better himself financially, I would wish him or her luck.

The lease negotiations were going well. I knew I needed a long time to get paid back the cost of what I wanted to do. I got a 21-year lease at 7½ % of the gross with a cap at a million dollars. The top rent was $75,000 a year. I was amazed at how many people were stuck in the old rule that the west side was not the gold belt. Lincoln Center was the catalyst for changing all real estate value. I was convinced that I was born with a lucky star over my head. But I was still coming from survival, I was still that street kid.

Pat's dad suddenly had a massive heart attack. They rushed him to the hospital where he was in intensive care. I was at work when I got the call. I went straight there. I saw some of the family out in the hall. He had passed away. I felt a tremendous loss. It was complicated, I became numb, empty inside. Pat was on her way. This was going to be tough for her.

The Start of a New Company

The 1920 Restaurant Corp, DBA Herb Evans Investors, was coming out of the woodwork. I only wanted eight investors to put up $20,000 a piece. I had 50% and they had 50%. I had control of design and operation. I guess it's a cliché to say I wish I knew then what I know now.

I was flying high, I wanted what I wanted. I got a good contractor and we gutted the space. My design was all brick and exposed ductwork in a high ceiling, 250 seats, a full bar seating 20. All the brick had to be used. This was difficult because new brick could be delivered on pallets, used was just dumped on the sidewalk. I would go to a demolition site and buy what I needed.

Working at Lincoln Center gave me the advantage of knowing what to put on the menu. Curtain time was 7:00, 8:00 and 8:30 p.m. We would empty out by 8:30 and get ready for the big hit starting around 10:00 p.m. That was late supper, fun time. The bar was always packed.

The dining area was four steps lower level. The Broadway front was all archways with the upper section of hand-blown stained glass. The lower section of the arch was French door windows opening up to an outdoor patio.

Still working at Lincoln Center and running across the street to check on construction, leaving home at 7:30 or 8:00 a.m. and most times returning about midnight. Not a formula for a good relationship. Family life was definitely strained. I kept saying that this is going to change, I just need time.

Lincoln Center was sold out 95% of the time. The excitement and energy were constant, I was addicted to it. The Herb Evans Restaurant was almost completed. It was beautiful. Fred Staton, who I worked with the past three years, committed to coming with me. In 1966 Samantha was born, two beautiful daughters. Things looked good on the outside.

The restaurant was ready for a grand opening. We planned it perfectly to open with the Music Theatre at the State. I booked the reception, with Richard Rogers. We had klieg lights out front, lighting up the sky. The show was "Annie Get Your Gun", the curtain came down, and the crowd headed to us. It was black tie formal, a cocktail party. The giants of Broadway were there – Richard Rogers, Irving Berlin, Ethel Merman, John Raitt, just to name a few. The press was snapping pictures. We opened on the highest note possible. One problem – there was nowhere to go but down.

Alex Botero, Yehudi Menuhin

A regular at my bar across from Lincoln Center, Alex Botero, the first violinist with the N.Y. Philharmonic, was sipping a scotch rocks at the bar. Yehudi Menuhin, one of the world's great violinists, just came in, he saw Alex and took his violin out and gave it a quick zing. Alex took his violin out and answered him. You could hear a pin drop. This was one of those magic moments. Yehudi hugged Alex and said, "My colleague!" After that, every time I saw him Alex said, "You heard him, he called me a colleague."

Herb Evans

Under Construction

The Herb Evans Restaurant was under construction. One of the partners was a member of the Sommeliers Society. They were having a private dinner with special wines paired with each course. My partner, Mac Bennet, thought it would be a good experience for me to attend as his guest.

I had never been a guest at these kinds of affairs. I felt totally uncomfortable and out of place. I worked as a waiter at affairs like this, I was perfectly at ease behind a bar or working a dining room, but I wasn't ready to be sitting with multi-millionaires. My life was moving too fast.

I talked myself into playing this role, I was determined to pull it off. I was seated next to Edward Albee, the hot new playwright on Broadway. He turned to me and asked, "How is the construction coming on your new place?" Just that turned everything around for me. I was known.

At the end of the evening, he asked if I wouldn't mind showing him the rest of the site. We grabbed a cab and went over there. I had the key, and we looked around. He made a couple of good suggestions. I got more out of that evening as far as my own growth than anything before that.

Edward Albee, nominated for a Pulitzer Prize. That was something!

The Herb Evans Restaurant

Outside:

Corner of Broadway and Sixty Fourth Street; 26,000 used brick, random patterns; 185 feet of front on Broadway; 18-foot-high arches with French windows, hand-blown glass; opened up to a sidewalk café.

Inside:

Two hundred seats, solid custom oak tabletops, exposed ductwork painted out in high ceilings. A 6-foot diameter custom designed gas-lit chandelier, always on. A canopy from the entrance to the curb, held up with brass poles, always shined.

Vincent Sardi's was the famous restaurant in the middle of the Broadway theaters. My place was across from Lincoln Center. We were called "The uptown Sardi's"; when a show opened, the place to be to read the reviews was Sardi's or Herb Evans's.

Stepping inside the front door into the vestibule to catch the cold air, then the inside entrance to the coat check and the 40-foot bar carved out of mahogany slabs. Greeted by the Maître d' and night manager, Fred Staton. Lots of excitement, always an opening in one of the shows – The Opera, New York City Ballet, The New York Philharmonic, The Beaumont for drama.

Danny Quinn, the local detective from the Sixty First Precinct, was always there looking out for us. Danny's food and drink were on the house. He never abused the unwritten law, like bringing a guest in. He made sure I got home safely at the end of my night. Danny was a big man. He was known, but always subtle, graceful in his movement around the bar.

One time while I was talking to him, he spotted a guy lift a purse that was on the floor. The bar was crowded. This guy grabbed it with the handle of his umbrella and let it slide down. It was slick and obviously professional. I didn't see it at all. Danny just excused himself and stopped the guy in the vestibule. Didn't even arrest him, just took the purse and the umbrella, told the guy to stay out of this neighborhood. The guy was lucky to get out of there. Danny put the purse back, no one saw anything, and we ended up with another umbrella. That's how smooth Danny was, glad he was on our side.

We ran three menus – lunch, dinner, and late supper. When you called, we asked your curtain time, either 7:30, 8:00 or 8:30 p.m. We put that on the table. Our patrons could relax when they knew we were aware of their timing. If it was raining, we gave you a poncho raincoat. We were all about service. At 11:00 pm, late supper, people came pouring in. It was the place to be.

Herb Evans

Robbery

At the restaurant, the layout of the floor plan as you enter to the left, the main dining room is four steps down, then another ten steps down to the bathrooms.

Between the bathrooms is a door to the office that's another five steps lower. At 2 a.m. we took the cash from two registers in the drawers to the office.

Al Lewis, my night closing man in charge, carrying the two cash trays, was opening the office door which swings out towards him. Just then a guy comes out of the men's room and puts a gun to Al's back. "Hand over the money."

Al turns around and hands the money trays, the guy falls back on the stairs. All the money spills onto the floor. The guy panics, drops a paper bag and his gun. Al closes the door to the office. The door sweeps the money, the gun, and the paper bag into the office.

The guy runs out the front door and down the street. The bag contained handcuffs. This guy lost his gun and cuffs and didn't get a dime.

I was standing at the bar with Fred Staton, my

night manager and Maître d'. We had no idea what just happened when Al came up and told us this bizarre event. We couldn't help but laugh. We all had a drink and locked up and called it a night. I told Fred to go home, Al and I would wait for the cops. We wouldn't have called them, but the gun might be evidence in another crime.

Fred Staton

Fred Staton, my Maître d' and night manager, was throwing a party for his sister. She was returning from England where she had great success as the jazz singer Dakota Staton. He invited me and Pat to come up. I had never been exposed to prejudice and didn't realize how dangerous Harlem could be.

Dakota was cast to play Billie Holiday in the movie about her life. Hollywood found out that Dakota was a member of the Black Panthers and she was dropped from the film. Well, Pat and I bounced into Fred's apartment ready to have a good time. The music stopped and one of the guests called Pat a white devil.

Fred was really upset. I told him it was okay, but we left. It was an eye-opener for us.

The next day Fred and I sat down and talked about what we could do, even if it was just a little. We started a training program to get kids off the streets. Fred was actively recruiting up in Harlem. It wasn't easy, but we thought no matter how small a difference, it was worth it. That was an important experience for me.

Herb Evans

Chagall

Marc Chagall, the famous artist, was working on a huge mural over the entrance of the Metropolitan. I saw him coming down from the scaffold. He was coming across the street, he went past us and into The Ginger Man. We were disappointed, but it wasn't a couple of minutes and he came into our place.

He went right to the bar and got a drink. I told him we were honored to have him as a guest. He had on white coveralls splashed with paint of all colors. He told me the Ginger Man thought he was a bum and turned him away!

I had a lot of fun teasing Patrick O'Neal, the owner of the pub. I never let him get over that one.

Life in Another Dimension

To write, to draw, to make music, to appreciate, adds to another dimension to life.

When looking at a painting and feeling the color, the movement of the brush, seeing a lost picture deep in the flowing paint;

or listening to a full orchestra, each musician holding their part like a puzzle that interprets what the genius composer hears – it lifts me off the earth as it fills my head with soaring sound;

or watching a ballet that was choreographed by the great Balanchine, in awe of the strength, the work it took to achieve, counting my blessings to be spending three years working in Lincoln Center;

or watching a ballet of water to appreciate the sculptures of Henry Moore, Leopold Lipschitz, no matter where you stand you feel the energy of creativity.

I look up and see Marc Chagall painting a mural above the entrance of the Metropolitan Opera House. He is on a scaffold and covered in paint. From the distance he looks to be in the mural.

Just prior to this incredible time, five years working different bars, clubs, restaurants in Greenwich Village. Surrounded by the free-flowing energy of artists like Bob Dylan, Harry Belafonte, George C. Scott, Jason Robards, Dustin Hoffman. New young actors like Al Pacino, Robert De Niro. The streets were crackling.

I could walk into any club or bar and catch a little of the next sensation. I was a local, known as Herb the bartender. It was another world from East Twenty Fourth Street in Brooklyn.

Writing about this now is exciting. I was definitely born with a lucky star over my head. It's easy to slip away from this rich tapestry, but to write brings it front and center. To share definitely takes you to another dimension.

Prior to Greenwich Village, four years on a submarine, a different rhythm but nevertheless, rich in the depth of family. No doubt about where you belong, this was your choice.

Possibilities

When I look at my life, I feel that anything is possible. Almost every restaurant I designed and opened, I was told by potential investors they didn't think I had the location or parking required to be successful. Even the location on Broadway, the East Side, was the place to be. Of course, after I got these places opened I was told it's because I had a great location.

Sam was three years old, Shelley was six. When I got to Los Angeles, they were living in Century City with their mom and Arnie, Pat's new man. I will never forget the first day they came down by themselves in the elevator. Sam was shy and hesitant, and Shelley was holding her hand so gently, telling her, "It's Daddy." Then there were lots of hugs and kisses.

I became a weekend dad. The pony rides on Pico Boulevard was the place where all the dads were. It was the meeting place. I kept thinking about the possibility of turning this around, opening a business, getting a home, meeting a woman and having the kids with me. I never doubted that this was going to happen. Anything is possible.

Alice's Restaurant

Finishing up construction on Alice's Restaurant, meeting purveyors, talking to inspectors, working a skill saw. Learning a big lesson, never use a power tool without your full attention.

While talking to an inspector I reached down to get the skill saw and didn't notice that the safety guard was not covering the blade. You guessed it, I stuck my hand into the blade. The power was not on but the blade was still spinning. I stopped the spinning but tore my right hand up. My partner Bob saw what happened and grabbed a t-shirt that was lying on the floor.

Fortunately, Alice's was right down the street from UCLA. We ran there, and I walked in with my hand wrapped in a blood-soaked t-shirt. The doctor on duty was also a medical professor and had a bunch of med students there. He was using this as a great learning opportunity and was talking to them as I was almost passing out. "Notice," he said, "a saw cut is messy, not as neat as a knife."

I didn't know whether to laugh or cry. They were all hovering over me to get a good look. Luckily it looked a lot worse than it was. After they cleaned it up, stitched the deep part, and wrapped it in bandages, I was good to go. I used this on my employees more than I should; it was a running joke – "Yeah, we know, you have your blood in this place."

Opening in 1970 put us in the middle of the protests against the Vietnam War. Being named for the song by Arlo Gutherie, it was often assumed we were part of the movement.

While we did have brownies on the dessert menu, they weren't hash brownies.

In the neighborhood, the protests were pretty intense. The Bank of America was fire-bombed, Westwood Blvd. was packed with students from UCLA.

We were being watched by the authorities. Most people thought we were a meeting place and involved in the politics of the time. It was really bizarre because Bob and I were not involved in politics at all.

We were just trying to survive the restaurant being under-capitalized. Our working capital was limited to the money in the till.

Our cash flow was day by day.

Then, a stroke of luck – Lois Dwan, the food critic of the L.A. Times, came in. She wanted to interview me. Bob was off, so most of the article was about me and how far from the formality of Lincoln Center and my New York restaurant I had come.

Alice's had a line out the door as soon as the article appeared. It created some friction between Bob and me. But what the hell, we were a hit.

A few of our service people were exchange students from Iran. One was Mustafa. He carried himself like royalty. I called him King Mustafa. He told me he was not Iranian, he was Persian.

A few of the other students from Iran said the same thing. Politics was not talked about. We were focused on food and service. But there was a political undercurrent – you couldn't get away from it. One time Mustafa took a ten-day leave. A strange thing occurred, a couple of men came in and asked if they could talk for a moment. We went up to the office. They showed me their identification, FBI. They wanted to know where Mustafa went and how long he worked here. I told him he was a great waiter and always respectful to guests and fellow workers.

Well, Mustafa never came back and I never saw him again. Employees come and go, especially exchange students, but this was different. I think about him from time to time.

with Richard Rodgers

with Ethel Merman

with Irving Berlin

with John Raitt on the right

with Eve Abbott and Van Johnson

S.F. Examiner—Page 41
ne 6, 1966

Earl Wilson

Rave About Ethel but Do... Send Roses

NEW YORK POST, WEDNESDAY, JUNE 1, 1966

Annie's Back

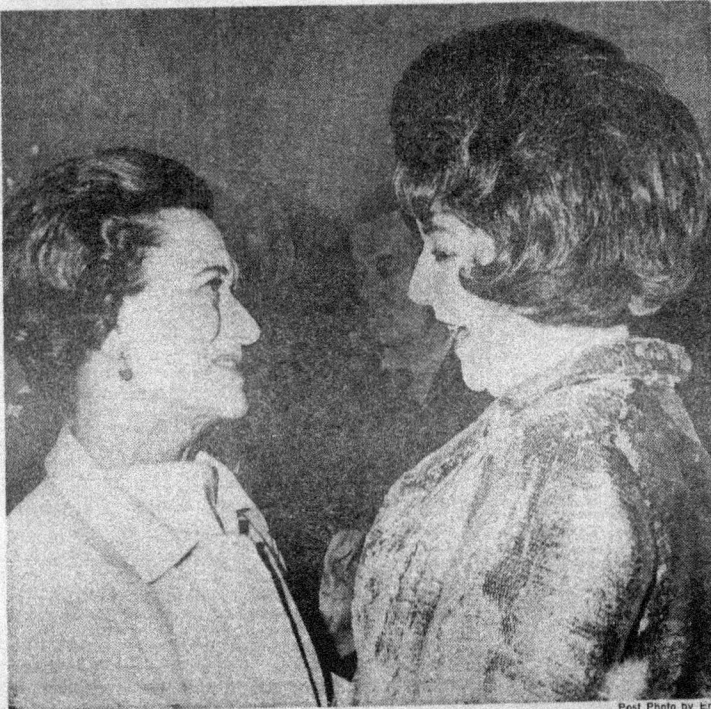

Post Photo by Engel

The Duchess of Windsor greets Ethel Merman at a party at Herb Evans' Restaurant, Broadway and 64th St., after the star opened in "Annie Get Your Gun" at the Lincoln Center Music Theater. Richard Watts' review is on Page 66, Earl Wilson's column Page 22.

1970's

Cezar Chavez Fundraiser

I catered a fund raiser for Caesar Chavez. He formed a union for farm workers and started the boycott movement to stop buying grapes. A valued possession of mine is a framed personal letter from him expressing thanks.

Herb Evans

Taking a Break

I took a drive up the coast for 3 or 4 days the first time I got out of LA. I didn't expect this, but it was a life-changing experience. The question I asked myself was, "Am I ever going to settle down?"

As I drove north a sadness came over me. I couldn't understand what this was. I had the hot new trendy place, money was coming in, bills were being paid.

Just past Santa Barbara, I pulled over in a turnout. The ocean was sparkling with the sun bouncing off the water. I had nothing to be sad about, but there it was, and it wouldn't go away.

I kept driving north. As I got past San Luis Obispo I felt as if a weight was flaking off me. I was feeling free. Now the coast was getting windy. It was the most beautiful view I ever saw. I'd better pay attention, this was getting scary. A mistake on this road would end it all.

I started to think about how fragile life is. I wasn't sad anymore, I was focused on the road, excited to see where this was taking me.

I was getting tired. A sign said "Big Sur, 26

Miles". I got to a place called Deetjens Big Sur Inn.
To say it was rustic was an understatement, but I
was lucky they had one empty cabin. I thought I
would take a nap, but I was too wired from being in
a strange place. The girl at the desk told me that a
mile up the road there was a place called Nepenthe.
They had a good bar and an excellent burger. Sounded like just what the doctor ordered.

I pulled into the parking area and followed the
signs up to this huge deck. The view was breathtak-
ing. There were a lot of people and a live band. This
was the last thing I was expecting.

A girl holding a tray with glasses of champagne
seemed to be floating across the deck with the grace
of a ballet dancer. She came up to me and offered a
glass. I reached into my pocket and dropped a couple of bucks. She waved it off. "There's no charge,
this is the Leo party," and she floated away.

That was the first time I met Holly Fassett. She
would play an important role in my life years later
when her father, Bill Fassett asked me to run the
place.

I asked someone else what was going on.

"They have a party for the astrological sign every
month," they said.

I happen to be a Leo. It was magic.

I didn't have any opinion about astrology, but
being a Leo I said, "Sounds good to me."

There were concrete steps above the deck, lots

of colorful pillows tossed casually. They called this the bleachers. Tara, the girl I was talking to, kept running off to dance but always came back. She was strong and confident. She was like seeing the view for the first time. She was Big Sur.

I told her about Alice's Restaurant and the success we were having. She was not the least impressed.

There was a feeling that this girl could live in New York and be just as confident. She was a survivor, like me. I had to go back to the inn and get some sleep. As I was leaving I said, "I'll see you again some time."

She said, "Sure, anything is possible."

The next morning, I thought I'd better start back. The drive was filled with that experience of Nepenthe and Big Sur. When I got to Alice's I couldn't shut up about it. Bob thought I'd lost my mind. I thought so too.

Bob and I were like a perfect storm, two large egos trying to create a picture on the same canvas. We were brothers but had to move on. The best way to handle this was to open another place. Out of the blue, I called a real estate company in Carmel. An agent, Hank Adams, answered. I told him I just wanted to somehow get back to Big Sur. I knew I must have sounded strange. I told him about Alice's and that I didn't have money, and just thought if he had any ideas, he might call me.

Six months later, Hank Adams called. He said he was good friends with Bill Fassett, the owner of Nepenthe. He wanted to meet me.

I talked to Bill on the phone, invited him to come down. At that time there were shuttle flights out of Monterey to LA, $24 bucks round trip. I picked Bill up at the airport. Neither one of us knew what was next, talk about an improvisation. We were living in a world of possibility, not necessarily reality.

Bill proposed that I take over the management of Nepenthe. Bob and I saw this as an opportunity to solve our problem and separate for a while. We worked out an agreement that I would move to Big Sur for a year, with a contract that we would review in six months. This was crazy.

I was a New York, Brooklyn boy. Could I live in a rural, rugged country?

I didn't know, but I was willing to go all in. Bob was happy to support this move. We averted "the perfect storm", at least for a while.

I had to talk to Pat. I thought I would take the girls for three weeks. Sam was almost six, Shelley was nine. Bill Fassett would get me a house and I would get someone to take care of them when I was at work. I would fly down every weekend. I knew I could make this work. Pat was okay, she was trying to face up to her demons. Arnie, her boyfriend was beside himself. It was hard for him to understand that we as a family still cared for one another.

The girls were excited to come to Big Sur. We had a house in the woods. It was easy to find a some-one to take care of them while I worked.

The management of Nepenthe was all about getting it under control. Nothing was under lock and key. This is before computers. We were the only major place in town. Post Ranch and Ventana were not built yet. Getting ready for the move, finding a house, and planning my take-over, this was a com-plicated situation.

Lolly Fassett, Bill's wife, was really the visionary that made Nepenthe happen.

Before the Fassetts, Orson Welles and Rita Hayworth owned the property. There was just a log cabin. Orson and Rita never stayed there. Like so many people, they fell in love with Big Sur, but it takes a real commitment to live without the luxuries in their lives.

Bill and Lolly bought the property and moved into the cabin with their children.

Lolly's idea was to build the deck and serve tea and cakes for anyone that wanted to share that mag-nificent view.

That was in 1947, before anyone was dictating what you could do with your property. They hired architect was Rowen Maiden, who'd studied with Frank Lloyd Wright. With local craftsmen Frank and Walter Trotter, they built the building as it stands today.

They opened in 1949. You can imagine the stories. Thousands of people that have stopped over the years.

Nepenthe

I had an agreement to manage Nepenthe Restaurant in Big Sur. I owned Alice's Restaurant in Westwood Village in L.A. Bob Yuro was my partner. This is before Alice's in Malibu. Bob would stay in Westwood and I would be in Big Sur.

I didn't know if I would have any allies on the crew at Nepenthe, so, I asked Steve Copeland, a waiter who'd started with me at Alice's to come up and give me a hand.

In Big Sur, Nepenthe was the main employer, and almost everyone worked there in some capacity. It didn't take long for me to realize the responsibility that was present, the knowledge that you controlled their livelihood. In New York, if you let someone go they had another job, in some cases the same day.

I loved Big Sur, but it took a while to learn how to live here. Big Sur would chew you up if you didn't take steps to do the right thing. It's not like you could run out to the store if you didn't plan ahead. The closest market was twenty-eight miles away. If your heat was a wood-burning stove, you'd better have wood. It was over thirty-five miles to the nearest ER. At the hospital. If it was a stroke or heart attack, chances are you would die.

I kept thinking this is a long way from Brooklyn. There were moments I wanted to go back, but I felt down deep that I should hang in there. Maybe I'll be a mountain man with a New York accent.

I would fly down on weekends and check out Alice's and visit the girls. I was concerned how things were going. Bob was drinking and it was obvious this was not good.

It was good to separate, so Nepenthe was giving me more than I had to offer it. Shelley was eight and Sam was five, so my weekends were full. Alice's was busy and it was doing pretty well in spite of bad management. Bob was working on getting a location on the Malibu Pier.

We got the lease. Since it was a restaurant space, the permit process was fairly easy.

I met some crazy carpenters that were living on Partington Ridge in Big Sur. Casparian and Jeff Bishop were the leaders of this group. I brought Cas down to take a look at the space and see what he thought.

He and I were on the same page when it came to design. Gut the place, strip the floor down to the wood, pull the banquettes, pull all the lighting out.

It was an old-fashioned bar with red letherette and bad lightihng. I wanted to create the Alice's concept.

Eventually we rented a house on the Coast Highway that gave the crew a place to crash. I had to be
in Big Sur Monday through Friday.

Bob was telling Cas to do things like leave the
ugly carpet. Cas would call me, and I would say tear
it up. I could have been more diplomatic, but I got
my way.

Meanwhile the management at Nepenthe was a
struggle. In the seventies, business was not like it is
today.

There wasn't much I could do except try to control the operations. In the winter, mid-week we only
served lunch.

Bill Fassett was a great story teller. He would get
his buddies like the writer, Henry Miller, and they
would crack open a bottle of Courvoisier, then get
into a rowdy game of dominoes.

At the end of the month Bill would complain
about the liquor cost. I would remind him he and his
cronies would kill a case of Courvoisier and more.
He would just grumble.

Herb Evans

A Memory

A beautiful balmy evening out on the deck at Nepenthe. Checking on my tables to make sure they have what they need. It was going to be a full moon, just beginning to show itself from behind the ridge on the mountain across from us.

The sun was setting and the moon was rising. The Santa Lucia mountains jutting down to the sea slowly changing color. The mountains appear to be breathing as the colors change.

Everything is alive.

The moon is sits on the ridge of the mountain, and just for a moment at the same time the sun is setting on the calm ocean.

I walked over to table just outside the restaurant door.

The man sitting there was just frozen, staring at the moon. He said, "I never saw the moon look as beautiful as it does tonight, and I walked on the moon!"

This was Buzz Aldrin, the astronaut who went up with Neil Armstrong, July 20, 1969.

Herb Evans

Century City

I received an interesting call. Century City is an area four blocks by four blocks, developed on the flats of Beverly Hills. It was high-rise buildings of office space and condominiums. Avenue of the Stars had a Shubert Theater. There was always a Broadway show playing.

The call I got was from the owner of one of the high rises. He wanted to explore the possibility of opening a restaurant. Alice's Restaurant was just the theatrical concept that I felt would work if I had the right space and I could negotiate a sensible deal. My experience those three years at Lincoln Center was perfect for this challenge.

At Alice's Restaurant, the wrap party for "Coming Home" starring Jane Fonda and Jon Voight, an important anti-war film nominated for many Academy Awards. Jane was married to Tom Hayden, an activist well known to be the antagonist in the Chicago Seven responsible for disrupting the Democratic Presidential Convention.

Being close to history-making events got me more interested in what our government was involved in. Tom Hayden ran for the Senate and with Jane's backing raising money, he became a Senator from California. I was involved in catering quite a few political functions.

A Restaurant Moment

It was a balmy July evening. We were restless. Tara said, "Let's go out to dinner." Shelley and Sam were definitely into going out. Being in the restaurant business, surprisingly we rarely went out to eat. It was like we were in a party all the time, so it was nice to stay home.

There was a new place, just opened in Brentwood, not far from Alice's in Westwood, the "Bicycle Shop Café". We thought, let's give that a try. When we walked in, it was packed. Everyone wants to try a new place. We didn't mind waiting, we loved to people-watch. There were quite a few patrons who knew who we were because of Alice's, so it was nice to chat and visit. The girls saw some kids from school. Sam was a little shy, she was only eight, but she knew how to enjoy herself.

We finally got seated after about an hour. I was enjoying the décor, bicycles hanging from the ceiling, marble top tables and bar. I liked noisy, and it was that. The concept was casual and the menu was California, meaning lots of salads, burgers and seafood. As we were reading the menu, a waitress carrying about five dishes to the table next to us lost her balance and dropped the whole order. One of the dishes hit the corner of our table. The marble top was hard as stone and the plate shattered into what seemed like a million pieces. The place was crowded and noisy so most people didn't take too much notice. Sam stood up and was bleeding on the back of her ankle. Tara was always ready to jump into action. (One time we were having dinner at Ventana and suddenly she jumped up and had to step on top of a table. I had no idea what she was doing. There was a gentleman who was choking. She immediately administered the Heimlich and a mushroom came flying out of his mouth.)

Well, back to what was unfolding at the Bicycle Shop Cafe. Tara took Sam into the restroom and controlled the bleeding. Big sister Shelley was a calming influence. I was standing just outside the restroom. It was not too bad and we were still hungry. When we got back to our table, there were people sitting reading the menu! There wasn't any manager available. It seemed like if they ignored us, maybe it would solve itself. We were told it would be an hour's wait for a table. I felt like this was a Jerry Seinfeld episode. We left and went to Alice's. At that point we were laughing and thought nobody will believe this!

About a week later I got a call from the owner. He was so embarrassed. He invited us to come for dinner any time. When you go out to dinner, in some instances you are entering the unknown. Come to think of it, we are always entering the unknown.

Los Angeles Actors Theater

Ralph Waite, the artistic director, was starring in a TV series called *The Waltons*. It was in its seventh year. The money was great, but it was driving him crazy – here was an actor capable of performing Shakespeare doing the same role year in and year out. He was an old friend, and he helped us out on a number of occasions.

I would spend time listening to him bitch about playing John Walton, the father of the Walton family. He was getting $10,000 an episode. That was pretty good back then.

Ralph allocated $50,000 of his own money for the Los Angeles Actors Theater. The first play was *The Kitchen* by an English playwright, Arnold Wesker. The whole play was in a busy restaurant in the kitchen. Ralph wanted me to set the stage and Tara to direct the actors to mime the use of cooking utensils, broiling, sautéing, chopping, carrying trays, and general behavior in a busy restaurant kitchen.

I went to a used equipment place and made a deal to get the stainless-steel tables and equipment to create the reality needed for this environment.

It was hectic and had lots of energy. The story was every restaurateur's nightmare. It was challenging to get the movement of servers and bussers coming in and out, and the cooks and butchers moving with urgent energy. The crescendo of the play is a butcher that goes crazy and, with a cleaver, breaks the gas lines and water lines. This happens just when the dining room is full. I've had dreams of that happening. The kitchen in a successful restaurant is a high-powered, stressful place in motion all the time.

Opening night, we all went to Alice's to wait for the reviews. It was exciting, felt like New York. The play was well received by critics and the LAAT was off and running. Ralph was happy.

The next play was ambitious – Eugene O'Neill's *The Hairy Ape*. This was a difficult one to stage. Tara again was instructing the actors in movement and mime, and she also had a role. I was not needed this time but was supporting the effort. Ralph had a difficult job casting the lead actor. All of O'Neill's plays were tough to produce – O'Neill is tough to perform, and *The Hairy Ape* is one of his most difficult. There were only a few actors that were considered O'Neill performers: Scott, Robards, Lee J. Cobb.

Ralph finally got a Broadway actor, Mitch Ryan, who was a very strong Shakespearean actor and friend from Broadway. That made some local actors unhappy. There was always competition existing between New York and California. I must admit New York actors were a bit snobbish. Mitch was also a good friend and was in my restaurant on Broadway often. Ralph and Mitch were both going to AA meetings almost daily. It was not easy for Mitch, taking on a complex role and dealing with his own demons. *The Hairy Ape* opened to raves.

Ralph wanted to direct a film, and because his contract was ending, he was able to get the backing for a low budget comedic love story. He read a story in the L.A. Times about a homeless couple who lived on Fifth Street in downtown L.A.

Fifth Street was called "The Nickel". It was like the Bowery in New York. Ralph wrote the script. He created a real community amongst the homeless.

On the Nickel was funny and touching, but no one went to see it. The Waltons finally was canceled and was now in syndication. It was being shown almost every day. Money was rolling in.

Repertory theater was difficult to maintain. It took a real commitment and very little monetary reward. Ralph had been making good money on "The Waltons", and he was putting his money into supporting LAAT. I knew that couldn't last.

Ralph was involved in lots of worthy causes. He got me involved in most of them – Native American causes, Caesar Chaves, The Farm Workers. For some I just catered fundraisers. Anyway, Ralph did a few movies after that but he never had to work for a paycheck again.

Tara Comes to Los Angeles

At the opening of Alices, I invited Tara to come down to live in Los Angeles. It started as filling a need to make a home with her and the two girls, Shelley and Sam. She agreed.

There was no talk of marraige. The kids loved her and always went to her for everything. I decided to talk to Pat about our having the girls live with us.

I just asked her if she thought it would be better for them, nothing legal. Just what's good for the girls.

I told the girls that their mom would always be welcome anytime. It took a lot of courage for Pat to agree. It never occured to me that it was just as courageous of Tara to deal with this.

We were settling in to a strong family. Everything seemed so right. I had driven north on a break and stopped at Nepenthe where I met Tara. She was a country girl, and I was a city guy. When I left I said, "I'll see you soon."

She said, "Anything is possible."

The girls went out and found a place in Rustic Canyon, Santa Monica. It was a nice Cape Cod.

She got involved in the start of LAAT.

Shelley and Sam were doing good in school, and time was moving us along.

Five years later, Tara's older brother wanted to marry his girlfriend, Marty. Helmuth was younger than me, but seemed like my big brother. We never paid any attention to the years.

This was the life that I built together with Tara. This was the way I moved on from the city life in Brooklyn and Manhattan, to the life in Santa Monica and Malibu, and finally to a home in the wild country of Big Sur.

Yellow House Restaurant

Tara and the girls went looking for a house in Rustic Canyon, Santa Monica. I was busy with Alice's Restaurant. They found a nice Cape Cod on Sycamore Road, just two blocks from State Beach.

The timing was perfect, just before real estate started to appreciate rapidly. It was perfect for me. I would walk every morning down to the beach. Sam was in grammar school within walking distance. Shelley was in Pacific Palisades High School.

On my walk to the beach, I passed a space for rent that appealed to me. I decided to call, and the rent was really reasonable, the lease was perfect. So, the concept for The Little Yellow House was going through my brain. It was only fifty seats and six seats at the bar. I formed a small corporation, "Sandshell, Inc., DBA The Yellow House." Both Sam and Shelley worked there after school.

The Yellow House became the neighborhood place. We would get calls from parents that they had important places to go and their kids would be coming down. "Let them sign the tab and we'll be in to pay." We never had a formal policy of running a charge, it was something we did if asked.

We had silver platters, really stainless steel. We served a family style bacchanal feast, serving four to six persons. One was a seafood platter, one was a meat platter with ribs and thin slices of broiled steak, vegetables, and potatoes. We opened at 8:00 a.m., served breakfast, lunch and dinner.

I thought it was the best place I ever opened, but I said that most of the time when I opened a new place. But this was different. It was the center of the neighborhood in Rustic Canyon. The meeting, eating, drinking place. The canyon was mostly populated with artists, actors, writers, people in the movie business. It was packed almost all the time with people waiting to get in, except Monday night, for some reason I couldn't figure out.

Tara and I decided to do something different. We had a forty-gallon steam kettle that I got from a hospital being renovated. It was a great piece of equipment. Our soups were getting talked about and really popular.

We decided to get bushels of littleneck clams, steam them, and serve in a bowl, all you could eat for nine dollars, only on Monday night.

We weren't making any money, but Monday became the busiest night of the week. After about six months, we decided to cut the "all you could eat", and Monday stayed the busiest night. It became the thing to do: Meet you at the Yellow House for some clams and a pitcher of beer.

An example of how important The Yellow House was to the community is an incident involving one of the artists who was there every day. John came in one night and was on something. He became abusive to the bartenders and they wouldn't serve him. They called me, and I walked down.

As soon as I walked in, he started to yell and I got him out. He broke some glasses and a lamp. Kathy, the girl behind the bar, was pretty upset. I told her she could go home and I would cover her shift. I eighty-sixed John, that's restaurant lingo for "you're out of here".

After a week, some of the customers asked if I would give John another chance. I was not going to, I thought he was a risk. It could have been violent. A few more weeks went by. One of the guys made a drawing of John behind bars with the caption, "Free John". Then one night everyone had t-shirts on with that picture of John behind bars.

That was it, I said call him, and he came down and we had a party. He told me he was so sorry and apologized to Kathy.

The Yellow House was definitely more than just a restaurant.

Herb Evans

Tara – A Mime

Tara wanted to participate in a two-week class with Maximilain Ducrot, the son of Etienne Ducrot, a master mime who taught Marcel Marceau. The class was held in Boulder, Colorado. We talked it over with the girls, we were up to the challenge, we thought.

There were a couple of bumps in the road, one being my cooking. The girls were great. They reminded me of Tara's rules: definitely communication, no after school stuff, we had to know where they were at all times. This is before smart phones, that seems so long ago.

They always asked permission if they wanted to bring a friend or two to Alice's Restaurant. They would always have a tip for the server. When Tara got home she got into a mime group headed by Richmond Shepard. They performed in the Westward Playhouse and some TV shows. Tara did some work on a Diana Ross special.

Mime was definitely a limited audience type of performing art.

The Summer of 1976

The summer of 1976 I rented a house in Pacific Palisades. I had the girls. Shelley was fourteen, Sam was eleven. Tara came to live with us full time, and the girls loved her.

Tara and I were like a married couple. Her brother Helmuth was in love with her good friend Marty. They decided to get married. Tara and I thought we could join them. To us, it was like acknowledging a union that already existed.

Ralph was an ordained minister. He agreed to come up to Big Sur and perform the ceremony. It was a beautiful day and we set up the lawn of Tara's mom's house on Pfeiffer Ridge. Shelley and Sam were wearing long dresses, and the wedding was beautiful. I was surprised how nervous I was.

Serving food and drink, that made me comfortable. So I walked around asking everyone if I could get them something to drink or eat. Shelley came over and reminded me I didn't have to work the party. I laughed and said I'd try.

Alice's in Malibu was a success, and that's where Bob spent most of his time. It was a party.

I was in Westwood. Alice's also doing well there.

We decided to make it legal, Bob in Malibu and Herb in Westwood, and that worked perfectly.

Tara asked me what we were paying for rent in this house we were living in? Why don't we buy a house? I thought about that for a moment and said, "Take the girls on the weekend and look for one."

They found a nice cape Cod on Sycamore Road in Santa Monica on Rustic Canyon, just a block from the beach. This is just before real estate went through the roof.

Things weren't going well for Pat, she moved out of Arnie's house and got an apartment on the Beverly Hills Flats. I went to talk to her, I was worried about the kids. I asked her if she thought they would be better off with me. It was not a legal thing, we just wanted what was best. If she got herself together in a while, we could talk about it again.

I told the girls that their mom was very courageous in this decision and that she wasn't well. We would always have her over for holidays and visits. Pat went back to New York to visit her aunt. She wasn't doing anything sleeping on the couch. She called me and wanted to know what was wrong with her. I told her she was an alcoholic and needed help. That was not received well. In those days most people didn't look at addiction as a sickness.

Ralph said he would sponsor her in AA. He had been going to meetings almost daily for a few years.

I got her to meet him at Alice's.

She didn't show the first time, but he said that's normal. After that, she got into AA and was sober for the rest of her life.

Tara and I were trying for quite a while to get pregnant. We finally got checked out, the doctor said try moving back to Big Sur, and it worked.

In 1982, Kyle was born. It was a natural home birth in our hidden-away cabin. The whole family was there.

Tara was in control, ordering everyone how to behave. Eighteen hours of labor and then, a beautiful baby boy. Shelley was nineteen, Sam was sixteen, and I was forty nine.

Herb Evans

Teddy

I never had a dog before.

While walking in Santa Monica's Rustic Canyon, a dog started to follow me. He looked like part shepard and part wolf. I stopped and firmly said, "Go home." He backed up a little and just looked at me with huge, soulful eyes. He definitely didn't look threatening, so I just kept walking. He was still following, always keeping about the same distance. I went into my house and figured he would go away. I looked out a couple of hours later, and there he was. I still couldn't pet him, he would back up every time I put my hand out. I put some food out, and this went on for about a week. Finally, on a weekend, I was sitting on the deck in the backyard. He cautiously got close enough for me to pet him. He didn't sit or lie down, just stood there. I rubbed his back, it seemed like about thirty minutes, and he just collapsed.

That was it, he was our dog. Why did he choose me? I took him to a vet, got him checked out. I had to stand next to him with my hand on his head so the vet could examine him. The doctor said he was probably abused. There was no collar or any ID. We figured he was abandoned, pushed out of a car.

I named him Teddy. If he was lying down in the house and I wanted him to go outside, I didn't have to raise my voice, just say, "Go outside," and he would get up and go.

We had Teddy for a number of years. He grew old with us. I never considered myself a spiritual person, I was more, "what you see is what you get." But Teddy got me thinking maybe, just maybe, there are some things you can't see.

Teddy passed away a number of years age. I still think about him, and he comes up in conversation.

There's always a good Teddy story around the dinner table.

Pfeiffer Ridge

Hank Adams, the realtor that got me to Nepen-the, called. We were in the Cape Cod house in Santa Monica, and things were really good. Hank said, "You've got to come up and see this property." We went up to visit Tara's mom and fell in love with the property, 26 acres on the ridge back a mile up, facing the ocean. The price was right, there wasn't any infrastructure, and we didn't have the money to develop it with a house, roads, water, and power. But that didn't stop us, we were always betting on the possibility, not a conservative way of living. This is before real estate started to appreciate by leaps and bounds. This was 1978.

We hired Jali, Tara's younger brother, to build the cabin. We found a spot that was hidden, couldn't be seen from the road. It took about a year, it was all redwood, beautiful. We were able to get electricity.

We also had a generator. Helmuth, Tara's older brother, was the genius heavy equipment operator – I mean he could cut a road at night and make it look like it was always there.

The property had a well near the Big Sur River. It

was 800 feet down to the river. We had to get a submersible pump. Electric power was already there. The tricky part was getting the pipe down there. The well was the only thing that was already on the property. We ordered a 12,000-gallon water tank and sat it on a concrete slab. Helmuth always knew when a building inspector was going to be in Big Sur. It was crazy, we had some close calls, there is no way you could do what we did today, but now we had water and power. What a luxury!

We designed the house and had an architect draw the plans. We wanted to get a permit and build a little at a time. When money came in, we bought material. When Jali finished the cabin, we moved in. We rented the Santa Monica house out, that covered the mortgage. We put that house up for sale and to my surprise, we were offered three times what we paid for it.

Sam was in middle school in Santa Monica, Shelley was at Palisades High. We stayed in Santa Monica for another year and a half until Sam finished school.

Shelley put in for a program called "Youth For Understanding", and at 16 years old went to the south of Sweden, a small town called Helsenborie.

The Yellow House had three waitresses from Stockholm. Shelley worked there after school and learned to speak fluent Swedish.

Sam volunteered to get bussed to an inner-city

school. I was proud of her motives but was worried about the experience. The bussing program was experimental, and at that time was not working.

At the end of the school year, Tara wanted to pick Shelley up and make it a vacation. It seemed like the only vacations we took were planned by Tara and the girls. I just went along for the ride.

We flew to Stockholm and rented a Volvo, drove down and got Shelley, took a ferry to Denmark, visited Hamlet's castle, and stayed in rented rooms in Luxembourg, Germany, France along the Riviera.

The car broke down in Cannes, France, and we had to stay there for a week waiting for a part for the car.

No one complained. It was beautiful. Shelley spoke fluent French and Swedish, Tara spoke fluent Spanish, I kept my mouth shut for almost the whole trip. I enjoyed getting up early before anyone woke and jogging along the Mediterranean.

Chefs from different restaurants were bargaining for fresh fish. It was bustling with life. I thought, "I could live here, the boys from Brooklyn should see me now!"

The part for the car arrived, so back on the road. We drove to Spain along the Mediterranean. We got to Barcelona. Tara wanted to get a guitar, and she tried out a few. She was really careful, listening to the tone. We went to a beach resort. I was really hot. Lying on the sand soaking up the sun, I was shocked when suddenly we were sprayed with cold water. That was a service that the hotel supplied.

It was time to head back home. The summer was over, Sam was starting Carmel High School. Shelley graduated from Palisades High. She decided she wanted to work for a year and decide what was next. She was smart, and I trusted her.

Friends and family were worried that she would never go back to school. I thought even if it was a mistake, she could handle that. She moved into a house with other kids in Monterey and worked in a couple of restaurants. She took some classes at Monterey Peninsula College.

I was getting more and more emotionally separated from Los Angeles. It was time to sell everything down there. I know I made some serious mistakes financially, but I was confident I could always create income.

Living in the cabin was great for me, but Sam was having a tough time. No matter what the weather, she would walk the mile down a dirt road to get the school bus to Carmel High, an hour commute each way. It's tough to be a teenager.

There was a dynamic between the kids from Big Sur and the kids in Carmel. Then there was Carmel Valley, the cowboys. I don't think anyone in the school system had their finger on the pulse of what was going on. I mean, from the outside this was a privileged, beautiful school.

with Bob Yuro in front of Alices Restaurant, Westwood, CA, 1969.

with Bob Yuro

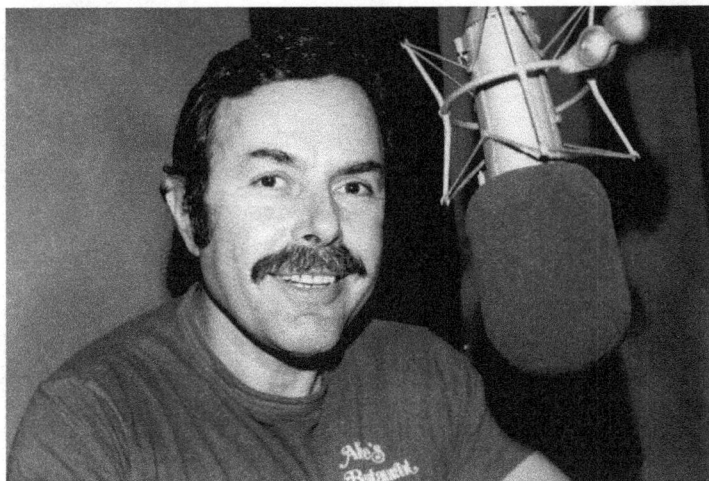

Do you know me?

American Express Company Restaurant Radio Campaign 1977-1978

Tom Hayden, 1971

Jane Fonda, 1971

with Jane Fonda and Tom Hayden, Alice's Restaurant

1980's

Herb Evans

The Treadmill

Finally, I was done with L.A.

I wanted a more peaceful life.

I sold Alice's, then The Yellow House.

The Cape Cod put us in a good position to finish the house in Big Sur. When Sam was 18 she decided to go down to San Diego. She got a job and fell for some Marine I never met. He got discharged and they went off to Florida. It wasn't long before she discovered this was not what she thought it would be.

One night they went out to a bar and some guy flirted with her. The Marine punched the guy out. Sam was horrified, being a nonviolent person. She called me immediately. I told her we would get her. I talked to Shelley, and we decided, or I decided, that I would get Shelley a flight to Florida and she could drive back with Sam. I told Sam to leave everything, just get in her car and drive back with her sister.

Shelley was a hero. She said, "Don't ever do that to me again. Do you know what it's like to be stuck in a car with a depressed teenager?" Well, we were all safe and were able to laugh. Thinking about that episode today, I can't believe I did that, put both my girls in harm's way. Today all I hear about is the crazies out there.

I got an idea to open a running store in Carmel. I thought I would do something different from the restaurant business. I had been jogging and my shoes didn't feel good. A light bulb went off in my head – a store with a treadmill to try out the shoes. I had the largest selection displayed on one wall. People in the business thought it was crazy to have such a huge inventory. To me it was my décor, the reputation we had was if you couldn't find it at The Treadmill, it wasn't available. We were doing okay, but trying on shoes, selling clothes just wasn't me.

Tara had her hands full with our new baby Kyle. I was a restaurateur, what did I know about a retail sports boutique? There was a store in L.A. that was really creative called The Front Runner. I went down to L.A. and talked to the owner, Pete. I asked him what would it take for him to give me an opening inventory and consult for a couple of days. Well, I gave him $2,500. For that, I had a Rolodex with all the numbers of contacts, Nike, etc. I got Jali, Tara's brother, to build shelving and storage. We were having fun with the design.

Shelley was working at a restaurant, The Tinnery, on Lover's Point in Pacific Grove. The Treadmill was fun, people were getting aware of the importance of health and fitness. Some friends thought it was crazy, that jogging was just a fad, it would pass. My thought was, once you become aware, you do not go back to being unaware. I was committed, running 10K's, 6.2 miles. I was on the committee in Big Sur to start the Big Sur River Run. The Run raised over one million dollars in thirty-five years. It supported the Volunteer Fire Brigade, the Health Clinic, it promoted local businesses to donate every year.

Meanwhile, Sam got a job in San Diego at the California Kitchen, a small chain. They had a computer that would give the orders to the bar and kitchen. There was a bartender, Steve, that instructed all the bartenders that he be the only one to service Sam's drinks. It was love from the start. Sam and Steve have been married 24 years, have three beautiful girls, and a lovely home in Campbell, California.

We talk at least four times a week.

Kyle's Birth

We were living in a beautifully cabin, hidden away on our property on Pfeiffer Ridge in Big Sur. Tara got our bed prepared with rubber sheets and a list of things the midwife wanted available.

Tara's water broke. This was going to be the day! All the family was there – her mom, Helen, sister Celia, Helmuth's wife, Marty, Jali's wife, Cindy and Shelley, our 19-year-old daughter.

Sam, our younger daughter, was on a summer trip with her Carmel High School class. There was no way to reach her.

It was a perfect July day, sunshine bouncing off the ocean and filling the cabin. Tara was the star of this show and took control with her usual strength – walking out on the deck, inside on the couch, not ready to get on the bed.

I just stayed at her side wherever she went. Her labor was about eighteen hours. She was giving orders and instructions. It was amazing how focused she was.

It was the first birth I was present for. The girls were born in Doctors' Hospital, New York City. With

Shelley I was just starting at Lincoln Center; with Sam, I was opening my first restaurant.

As controlled and planned as this event was, we never made it to the bed. We were sitting on the couch, Tara was complaining of a backache. I leaned over and whispered in her ear, "Let's push this baby out."

A few minutes later, out came baby. Maggie and Robin, the two midwives, were doing their thing. These women were powerful. I looked at Tara, and to me she seemed superhuman.

I never looked at babies the same way the rest of my life. Robin said "It's a boy!" I just wanted it to be alright. I kept saying under my breath and in my mind, "Please God, let everything be okay...and thanks for everything. Amen."

I never had any religious training, but I felt there had to be more than us, maybe a higher power. I sure didn't feel too powerful at this moment. Tara was so tired but still strong and knew exactly what she needed.

The lead midwife asked me to cut the umbilical cord. I was so nervous, my hands were shaking, I got it together as best could.

I remember looking at my newborn son thinking, "I owe you, kid!"

I'm sure it was more difficult than I make it sound.

Helmuth, Tara's older brother who has since

passed away, was a master craftsman. He made a bassinet out of redwood. He hung it from the ceiling with chains at the foot of the bed, tied to a line so we could swing him in the middle of the night. When he stirred, we pulled the line and he would swing to sleep.

Cindy was also pregnant that summer. She had a girl two days later. Marty had a girl a year later. We all lived on Pfeiffer Ridge – we were named "The Pfeiffer Ridge Rabbits".

Sam got home a few days after her brother was born. She was upset like only a sixteen-year-old is capable of.

Café Central

Kyle was 5 years old and smart. He was going to a preschool, "Cheer For Kids", so Tara was able to be the chef at Café Central, our new ventue in Carmel.

There were a number of babies born around the same time in Big Sur. The moms, including Tara, started a preschool on Apple Pie Ridge. It became so popular that it is now located on the grounds of the public school, Captain Cooper. Apple Pie is part of the school system.

In writing this memoir, I took a look at why I moved from one thing to the next. Designing a new concept in the service industry was not as hard. I loved literally sitting on the floor of an empty space and designing the flow of traffic. Every time I spotted a For Rent sign in an architecturally interesting building, I would pull over. But staying put and dealing with all the details – employees, staffing – that's the most frustrating.

Controlling a cash business before computers was almost impossible. I don't want to give the impression that everyone is stealing, not true. I do have some regrets not staying put and building a business, developing a loyal crew over time. The passion to stay with it wasn't there.

1986, still at Café Central, starting to look around; Don Bowen, a restaurant broker well known in Carmel, called, had someone interested and thought I might be willing to listen to an offer. Here we go again.

1990's

with grandson, Sylas Evans, 2014
photo by Kyle Evans

Negotiations With Smucker's

I was thinking about creating some income, a small fast food healthy restaurant. We'd serve mostly organic, steamed veggies, vegetarian soups, great smoothies. Tara designed the logo – "The Power Juice and Food Co." was born. We were just a little ahead of what people wanted. We were building a steady client base. There were customers coming in with their own containers for enough soup for the week.

One store couldn't show enough profit to make it worth the effort. But up to five stores and it would be great. We opened number 2 in Monterey on Alvarado street, then we opened a spot in the Del Monte Center.

Kyle was going to Carmel High, I usually was at Power Juice at the Crossroads by then. He walked down Ocean Ave. and got a job in a gallery doing shipping. I was his ride to and from home in Big Sur. He wasn't into team sports, but he was athletic, scuba diving, Frisbee, shooting pool.

When he was little I took him to Little League ball games, he was on third base one time and he ran off to center field. He called other kids out there. The coach went crazy. What it was, he spotted a gopher popping his head up to see all these little kids running out there. It was hysterical. Most of the parents saw the humor, but the coach didn't.

Anyway, back to Power Juice. One day, Tim Smucker of the Smucker's Jams and Jellies company called. They were interested in Power Juice.

I'd always heard their advertisement, "With a name like Smucker's it has to be good." This was a hundred year old company out of Ohio. We met with them at their plant in Salinas. It was really impressive.

This was a professional organization traded publicly. This was a possibility that set us up in a lucrative situation; we had to meet with their lawyers and ours. We entered into negotiations, it was exciting. They wanted Tara to be the nutritionist to supervise the opening of new outlets. I would supervise the layouts of new places. It was a perfect time for Tara to spread her wings.

Then, as fate would have it, Odwalla, the juice company, got hit with a huge lawsuit. The law was looking into controlling smoothies and fresh-squeezed juices. Smucker's, being a public company, got frightened and pulled out of our negotiations. They paid us generously for the consulting we did and for our legal fees. Odwalla had to pasteurize all their drinks. It was never proved what happened, they settled the lawsuits and we went on with our business. Our disappointment didn't last long, the fit didn't feel that good.

Kyle was now a senior at Carmel High. He applied for one college, Cal Poly, in San Luis Obispo. He was accepted to study electrical engineering. It seemed that Kyle would always get what he wanted. Of course, life does not work that way. I was always in awe of the way he dealt with whatever came at him. His strength for a young guy was logic. He would always say, "It is what it is."

Herb Evans

And Beyond

Herb Evans

Howie the Rat

My son Kyle graduated from the Art Institute of California in San Francisco. He and his girlfriend, Hillary, were moving to Reno, Nevada. He got a job as a computer artist designing gaming machines, what we used to call slot machines.

I had an old truck and wanted to help with the move. Living in Big Sur, it was good to have a vehicle that I could load up with firewood, just a workhorse whenever needed.

Driving from Big Sur to Oakland I thought I'd better check all the fluids and make sure this truck could make the trip. After loading up their vehicles and the truck, we headed for a gas station to check everything out.

As I was gassing up, a large rat jumped out of the front grill. He looked around for what seemed like a full minute. Then ran down the center of the street. This was a country rat that hitched a ride and now was in a big city.

I watched him as he ducked down a sewer, and I was thinking how was he going to get along with all the city rats?

My imagination was working overtime. I gave the country rat the name of Howie, don't ask why, it just seemed that a rat boxed in a situation like this would be Howie. I apologize to all the Howies out there. In my mind, Howie is a nice country rat.

Hillary, had graduated from Cal Poly with a degree in Animal Science. She thought that Howie wouldn't survive. She painted a picture of what he would be up against.

I said, "Since we're never going to know, let's think of a nice story."

I kept thinking of myself, coming from Brooklyn, New York, and now living in Big Sur. It wasn't easy, but I pressed through it. Lots of visitors fall in love with the beauty of the Big Sur Coast, the Santa Lucia Mountains cascading to the ocean.

The sun sets like you never saw before. If you turn your back to the setting sun you can watch the mountains change color. The colors merge slowly as the sun goes down. But the complexity of living in a rural area is just like living in a city.

Howie the country rat and Herb the Brooklyn street kid, it sounds crazy, but I related.

A Trip to New York

One summer a few years ago my kids took me to New York. We rented an apartment for a week on Fifty Seventh Street and Ninth Avenue. I had not been back since 1969. I told them what to expect. We flew into JFK, got a cab, the driver was on the hustle, he was going to give us a ride the long way. When he saw that I knew the city, we had a good laugh. There would be a lot of laughs after that.

I was talking to everyone, on the bus, the subway, cab drivers. It was a good time. Kyle was recording and taking notes. He was asking questions about everything. They wouldn't let me spend any money. This was a birthday present.

We went to Lincoln Center in the afternoon. Nothing was going on. I wanted to show them the kitchen in Philharmonic Hall. We walked in, there was a guy working on the refrigeration, he saw me and said, "Hi, Herb, what's up?"

That's perfect New York – forty years, and all I get is "What's up?"

We went to the Museum of Modern Art, the Museum of Natural History, also the Guggenheim, designed by Frank Lloyd Wright. I had heard that he hated the architecture of New York skyscrapers so the Guggenheim was a message to New York. Located on the conservative East Side on Fifth Avenue, a round building. The word was that he felt that New York was suffering from arthritis.

Being with Shelley, Sam and Kyle, I was seeing New York with new eyes and was just as excited to be doing these things as they were. They got tickets to a Broadway show, *Kinky Boots*. It didn't matter what the show was, just what was available. It was Broadway.

We got to see a Van Gogh exhibit at the Museum of Modern Art. Standing in front of his Starry Nights, it felt like you could walk right through the canvas and be in his world. I never saw paintings like that or felt like that before. I wished I had more energy, I would have stayed longer. But tomorrow is another day.

We went to the old block, East Twenty Fourth Street. There were a couple of kids sitting on the steps of one house looking at their cell phones. No clotheslines, no chalk marks on the street, no noise, no atmosphere, nobody calling anyone out of the windows. It seemed sterilized, clean, no character. I felt lucky to have had such a rich boiling pot experience.

My kids and I walked a few blocks to Sheepshead Bay. I wanted to show them "Joe's Clam Bar", the first restaurant I worked in. We went to the spot but – no clam bar.

The kids looked at me with a little skepticism. There was an old man sitting out front just staring out at the boats in the bay. I asked him what happened to Joe's Clam Bar. He was so excited, he had plenty of stories. He thanked me for asking. I think I made his day.

The kids couldn't get over this. It made our day, too.

Herb Evans

Crazy

Family and friends are just a phone away, my little computer gets text messages and voice mail instantly, just like everyone. This year children and grandchildren are spread out across the country. If I can't reach anyone or I don't get a response, I feel a little crazy. Fortunately, they all know how I am so it's not a problem.

Well, my granddaughter Julia lost her phone and my daughter Sam let hers go dead and my crazy mind created everything from science fiction to terrorist attack. I know this is ridiculous, but my heart was pounding.

On Christmas Day I was with my son and family in Big Sur. Up at the crack of dawn with my two grandsons, five-year-old Sylas and one-year-old Drake. They were so excited, they couldn't wait until Grandma Tara got up.

Their mom and dad were just getting up and we were sitting staring at the colorfully wrapped boxes under the skimpy tree. I was still okay at this point. I didn't expect to hear from anyone this early. But as the day moved on, no one else was aware that

Grandpa Herb was getting anxious, or to better describe it, getting crazy.

After brunch and opening the gifts, keeping busy cleaning up, the day was fading. Still no word from Sam. Getting ready to go to Nepenthe for their annual family dinner – this is by invitation, and I am fortunate to be on the guest list for about forty years. It was so beautiful at Nepenthe. We caught the sunset from the back deck. It was as dramatic as any I have ever seen.

By now, Kyle was aware of what I was going through and, being the really level-headed guy, he figured out what happened and was pretty good at calming me down. Sam called and texted and left a voice mail. I was fine, but still a little crazy.

Epilogue

Looking at Shelley, Sam, and Kyle today, I am in awe. Shelley is coming up on her thirtieth wedding anniversary and has a boy and girl. Sam is married twenty-five years and has three daughters. She will renew her vows this August. Kyle is married ten years and has two boys.

I found myself pulled, kicking and screaming, to write this memoir, and now I find I can't stop writing!

Herb Evans

A restaurant is show business, and the bar is the stage. A bartender is the talent, the stage manager, and the director all rolled into one. Everybody wants to know the bartender.

Herb's start in the business came at 80 Warren Street in Manhattan. Each day he'd be sent to a new venue, a new job. He always had work, because he never said no. Delivery boy, sandwich guy, griddle cook, waiter, or bartender. He'd get the gig and take the stage.

Herb finished his career at Nepenthe, one of the world's most beautiful sets. What lay between lies within.

www.ingramcontent.com/pod-product-compliance
Lightning Source LLC
Chambersburg PA
CBHW022004080426

42733CB00007B/471